Activate Your Power

How to Unlock Your Full Potential and Direct Your Own Success

Eitan Sharir

www.eitansharir.com

authorHOUSE®

AuthorHouse™
1663 Liberty Drive
Bloomington, IN 47403
www.authorhouse.com
Phone: 1-800-839-8640

First published by AuthorHouse 10/15/2010

ISBN: 978-1-4520-1679-5 (e)
ISBN: 978-1-4520-1677-1 (sc)
ISBN: 978-1-4520-1678-8 (hc)

Library of Congress Control Number: 2010906178

Printed in the United States of America
Bloomington, Indiana

This book is printed on acid-free paper.

Acknowledgments

This book was made possible by the support and encouragement of many people who have helped me along the way. I specifically want to thank the following people:

My wife, Meghan, whose unwavering love, support, and commitment has helped me to fulfill my biggest dreams and aspirations. I thank her also for her suggestions and creativity and for undertaking the task of editing this book to its current form.

My caring parents, loving sisters, and three beautiful children, who constantly remind me how precious life really is.

Lee Johnson for helping to transform the original content of this book into a well-presented and readable format.

And finally, all my clients, who inspired me through their focus, dedication, and actions to write this book.

Table of Contents

Foreword

In his description of man's archetypal journey, Joseph Campbell describes how we meet people along the way who are serendipitously important to our own personal mission.

On such a journey, I met Eitan Sharir.

He had asked my advice on doing business in Vancouver, and I had confessed that I was probably the wrong person to be talking to. I described the problems my business partner and I had encountered just a few years before in trying to get the local business community to accept the principles behind our latest book, *The Quest for the Corporate Soul*—namely, that true success in business is inextricably intertwined with personal consciousness and spiritual integrity. After sowing our seed on apparently barren ground, we eventually despaired of ever harvesting a bountiful crop.

However, within less than two years of arriving, Eitan had made an art of combining business with soul. He succeeded where we had failed. And not only did he succeed in attracting more business than he could handle, but his client testimonials were glowing in praise of his work.

I was fascinated. How had he done it? Suddenly, the teacher had become the pupil. And so, when Eitan asked me to help him get his ideas written down and published, I was more than eager to participate.

As the book *Activate Your Power* began to take shape, I got to know Eitan on several levels. First, he is one of the most persuasive people I have met. What makes him so good is how passionately he believes in what he is doing and how absolutely sincere he is in wanting to do the best for each of his clients.

Second, that passion for giving 100 percent extends beyond his working day. Eitan really strives to be a positive influence on everyone around him, not only involving them in his own enthusiasm and thereby inspiring a greater effort, but also inviting companionship on his own journey toward authenticity and higher consciousness. I have been privileged to share many evenings with Eitan and others who seek to light a candle rather than curse the darkness.

Finally, I have shared with Eitan that level of vulnerability and admission of imperfection that intermittently reminds us of our own humanness, and—if heeded—leads to humbleness and authenticity. We have taught each other and learned from each other. My own greatest gift in helping Eitan with his book is that it has also helped fulfill my own purpose of leaving this world a better place than it was when I came into it.

Whether you read this book in your corporate persona, striving to be both successful and ethical, or whether you read it as an individual seeking your highest self, I sincerely believe that *Activate Your Power* will be a valuable, positive catalyst in your life.

Lee Johnson
Author of Penguin Books #1 best seller
How to Escape Your Comfort Zones,
and author and co-creator of
The Quest for the Corporate Soul

About This Book

This book is about power and choices. More precisely, it's about choosing to reawaken the power that lies within you so that you can achieve a more meaningful, purposeful, and fulfilling life—life at home, life at work, life in general. All of us possess a natural and authentic power that we can access at will when we know how. It is not reserved for only a few lucky or chosen ones; it's held by all and available to all. As we learn how to access, or "activate" this power, the quality of our life experience transforms to something higher, bigger, better.

We humans have been created with the capacity for higher consciousness, which not only enables us to conceive our dreams and aspirations but also to pursue them with creativity and determination. With access to our innate power, we can change our own lives as well as improve the world around us. It is, therefore, our responsibility to use our power wisely and not waste it on useless distractions that sap our energy and create destruction and unhappiness.

Activating your power begins with you. It begins with a choice that you, that I, that we all need to make if we truly want to improve the quality of our life, our success, and our happiness. It's a choice that transcends mere survival and catapults us to a level of experience that is inspiring, abundant, joyful, and fulfilling.

This book was born from a personal wake-up call that I received in my early thirties—a serious call to action that profoundly changed my life and how I experienced it. Following that incident, I developed a fascination with the human condition and began to immerse myself in the study of human dynamics. Soon, my fascination grew into a passion that propelled me to explore the real meaning and purpose of life.

I observed and studied thousands of people from all walks of life, socioeconomic levels, and communities—people with different nationalities, belief systems, cultures, and backgrounds. It quickly became clear to me that despite all their diversity, most people share a common sense that something is missing from their lives.

This discovery, combined with my disillusionment with my own culture's popular formulas for success, prompted me to delve deeper into this common human experience in search of answers. I wanted to know what it was that people were lacking; what exactly was missing from their lives? And then, I wanted to find out how to get it.

In this book, I share what I have discovered. By making sense of these discoveries and "connecting the dots," you will gain a true sense of how aspects of your life fit together. You will learn how to harness and activate the powerful life energy that is available to you now, improve your relationships at work and at home, and live a more meaningful and successful life (by your own standards). You will be given the opportunity to explore your own feelings and attitudes, or put into practice new tools, through short, practical exercises scattered throughout the book and marked with the symbol ❖. The purpose of this book is to help you, the reader, achieve the life that you want.

I do not profess to have all the answers or to know the only way. I believe that there are many ways or paths to success and happiness. What I have outlined in this book is a way that I believe is practical, workable, and most important, achievable.

I invite you to activate your power now, for your sake and for the sake of those around you.

I wish you every success.

Eitan Sharir

Part I

Harness Your Energy

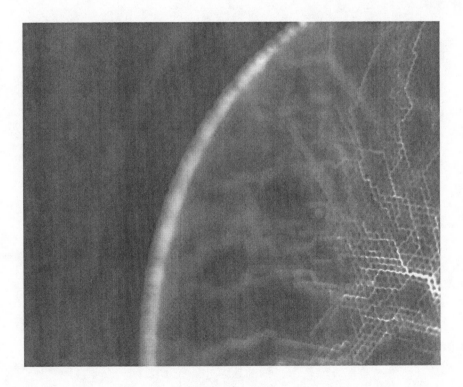

Chapter 1

Listen to Your Wake-Up Call

My Own Story

For most of my life, I was glad to be normal. Society taught me that to be the same as most people was good and safe; others would like me, and I would live a happy life. This belief influenced most of my choices and actions and, without my conscious awareness, also instilled fear and self-doubt in me for many years. I worked so hard to please others, to get the approval of others, and to be accepted that I lost touch with my true self. I became "accepted" rather than *real*.

I worked hard and played hard, got married and had many friends. After earning two university degrees in commerce, I worked even harder, growing increasingly successful and, at the age of thirty-one, became managing director of a company specializing in retail information technology.

Life was good. I was following a "normal" and predictable path.

People said that I was a high achiever who had it all: an enviable career, a good family, my health, and a great future ahead of me. In order to be normal, I looked brave and strong and didn't show anyone that I wasn't perfect. But, despite what everyone said—and despite what I might have projected on the outside—inside, I always had a whole collection of fears that I wasn't sharing with anyone. Fear of failure. Fear of not making it. Fear of not being smart enough. Fear of not being a somebody. Fear of success. Fear of death. Fear of people finding out that I was not perfect. *Fear of...*

At that time, my life was mainly driven by external events, circumstances, and situations. What happened on the outside had a large influence on what happened on my inside. If people liked me,

I felt great. If people didn't like me, I felt concerned, even rejected. I was very attached to *things*, and the mere thought of anything being taken away produced stress and more fear.

And then, something devastating happened that changed my life forever.

One of my friends, Peter, was an ultra marathon runner, extremely fit and healthy, with a great attitude about life. He had a wonderful wife and two young children, and it seemed that nothing could be more perfect than his life. Then, one Friday afternoon at work, I got a phone call, telling me that doctors had diagnosed Peter with advanced cancer of the colon. They'd found a huge lump that had to be removed immediately.

When I heard the news of my friend's illness, something important was triggered inside me and became the catalyst for a serious evaluation of my own life. The rest of that Friday, my mind and heart were in turmoil as I went through an intense period of self-confrontation.

The next day I took the time to sit down in a quiet place and ask myself a series of profound questions that would later transform my whole existence.

What is life all about? Who am I? What am I doing? Why am I doing it?

I looked hard at my current life, asking myself questions about all aspects, such as my friends, my spouse, my social situation. I had a good rapport with most people I knew but realized that many were acquaintances rather than friends. A sense of obligation rather than a deep connection shaped many of these relationships. I saw then that I needed to form new connections with people whose mind-set and purpose were more similar to my own.

I next considered my work. By society's norms, I was highly successful, and yet, somehow, something was missing. I was professionally as committed as ever but felt that I was destined to do something that was better suited to my natural talents—something that would tap into a greater power that I had. This power, however, had yet to be discovered.

I then asked myself the biggest question of all: *What should I do with the remainder of my life?* Should I continue as before, secure in my comfort zone, or should I seriously consider something else? The answer to this question did not come as quickly as the others.

I woke up on Sunday in a cold sweat. This was scary. What about money? What about my security? What about my position as managing director? A little voice on my shoulder whispered, *If you leave what you've got now, you'll have to give up all those perks and incentives: the company car and all those wonderful things that you've worked so hard for. Don't do it!*

Escaping from My Comfort Zone

I suddenly realized that all the wonderful things I'd earned had become my prison walls. My attachment to my title and position, to what my friends would say, and to accumulated material things was causing me to feel comfortable on the one hand and insecure on the other. I was afraid to confront the most crucial question: *Why should I change?* After all, my life was fine as it was.

I came up with other questions, the what-if's: *What if I lost all my things? What if I couldn't find a better job and ended up humiliated? What if, what if?* Clearly, my inner voice was trying to justify why I should *not* change.

Once I understood what the fearful little voice was doing, I no longer gave in to its doubts. Instead, I told it what *I* was about to do.

Your comfort zone can become your prison.

I realized that I could bypass my fears if I could consciously put them aside. And so, I visualized myself managing just fine with money issues, with what people might say, and with any other potential obstacles that might arise.

I asked myself, *If I could do whatever I want to do, without restriction, what would that be? What do I really want to do with my life? What would be the most meaningful?*

All Sunday, I contemplated my life and searched my soul. I wrote pages upon pages of ideas and insights as they came through from somewhere deep inside me. What eventually started streaming in was that the most meaningful and inspiring way for me to live my life would be to work with people as a catalyst to help them awaken to the power that lies within.

An incredible surge of energy flowed into me and filled my entire being with a sense of deep knowing. I felt inspired, energized, and liberated—even though I hadn't done anything yet. It was as if something inside me shouted, *This is it!*

I realized that the feeling of liberation that I was experiencing came from breaking free from the prison that I had created. The inner voice (my prison warden) was no longer running the show. I was! That was my first real experience of freedom.

In a flash, I understood that from then on, I had the freedom and the *power* to choose. I could truly choose how to respond, how to react, how to behave, and how to live my life. I could see so many new possibilities. This realization was one of the most inspiring moments of my life.

Monday morning, first thing, I went to meet with the chairman. I sat down and told him the whole story about Peter and poured out everything I had thought about over the weekend. Then I resigned and decided to move on.

I was moving on to live my purpose.

Why Hadn't I Acted Before?

I believe that the thoughts that had preceded my resignation had been hovering in my mind for a long time but hadn't risen to the surface. My vague feelings of discomfort were not yet crystallized, and because I felt that so many things were still attached to my job, I had avoided confronting myself and doing something about it, until the news about my friend.

Before that moment, I had asked myself challenging questions like: *Imagine that you have twelve months left to live. What would you do with the rest of your life?* But it was only a theoretical and intellectual exercise. I wasn't ready to confront it head-on.

But now I'd received my wake-up call, and it forced me to face things and do something about them. Less than three months after resigning, I started a new business.

Seven months later, my friend Peter passed away. I still thank him for his strength, courage, and inspiration.

Who Was in Control?

One of my greatest realizations was that before my wake-up call, most of my life had been determined largely by outside influences and not just what we commonly understand to be outside influences—advice from friends and family or perceived financial pressure. The outside influences issuing the orders I was taking were my own thoughts and emotions. I was so attached to my thoughts and emotions, I believed that I *was* my thoughts (whatever they were) and that I *was* my emotions (whatever they were).

This meant that when I had positive thoughts and feelings, I was happy—and when my thoughts and feelings were not positive, I was unhappy. I was allowing myself to be controlled.

The most frightening part of it all was that most of these thoughts and emotions would just arise as if out of nowhere, without me having much control over them.

Outside events would happen, which would trigger my thoughts, which would then stimulate my emotions. This process in turn energized more thoughts, which then heightened the emotions. Meanwhile, I felt just like a puppet on a string: vulnerable, powerless, and dependent on outside forces. But, armed with my newly awakened knowledge that I had the power to choose, I could see another way. Being so susceptible was no longer even an option.

> *Deep inside us is something valuable, worth listening to, worthy of our trust, sacred to our touch. Once we believe in ourselves, we can risk curiosity, wonder, spontaneous delight, or any experience that reveals the human spirit.*
>
> —e e cummings

And so I set out to change my relationship to my thoughts and emotions. Of course, I still had thoughts and feelings, but instead of following them blindly, I started to analyze them and then make choices of how to respond.

I was determined not to be a powerless victim of circumstance, driven by fear and a constant sense of vulnerability. Instead, I would operate with confidence, courage, and liberty.

What Do You Need to Wake You Up?

Since you are reading this book right now, you can probably identify with how I was before my wake-up call—not overly happy but not unhappy enough to make the shift.

What is very clear is this: *you don't have to wait for a disaster to strike in order to get your wake-up call.* You can take action **now** to change your life, but your motivation must come from within.

You can kick-start your own wake-up call.

You make your own choices in your life. If you are really serious about creating a more meaningful and successful life, both for you and for those whose lives you touch, the time to start is now.

The best way to begin is by examining your life as it is now. How are you experiencing life? What is your driving force? How does your own perspective affect your life?

Understanding What Drives Us

Human behavior is both fascinating and complex. The study of it helps to understand what drives people to do what they do. It also helps explain what stops people from pursuing the lives to which they truly aspire.

In order to move beyond our own limitations and be in a position to make good decisions, we need first to become aware that there is more than one way to view and, therefore, experience the world around us. We will now look at two different perspectives and the key driving motivators in each of those worldviews. It is important to remember that these perspectives are neither "good/bad" nor "right/wrong," but rather, ways of looking at the world through different lenses. For now, we need simply to understand that our way of looking at the world influences the experience we have of it, and that, moment-to-moment, we all make a choice to see things *horizontally* or *vertically*.

The Horizontal Perspective

At the foundation of each of the two perspectives is a raison d'être—the main justification for doing anything and everything. The main purpose for people who view life from the *horizontal* perspective is to survive.

Survival in this context is not necessarily at the basic physiological level (such as those explained in Maslow's Hierarchy of Needs: food, water, sleep, etc.), but rather the strong need to feel that we are coping with the uncertainties that are presented in daily life situations. People feel that they are coping well when they feel in control and when things are going their way. On the other hand, when they feel stressed, overwhelmed by work, or unable to complete their daily to-do lists, they generally feel that they are not coping very well.

Here is a typical example of a person living in the horizontal perspective, unnecessarily focusing on survival. Although universal, this example is a true account of a situation that I observed with a colleague of mine when I was still working in the corporate world.

Dan (his name has been changed to protect his identity) was a manager in a company that was undergoing some structural changes. Until the changes were begun, he came to work every morning and, mostly, did what was asked of him. His performance reviews indicated that he was a steady performer, and he got on relatively well with his colleagues. One morning, his immediate manager, the vice president, walked into his office and informed him that his department was going to be led by a new vice president, who would join the organization in four weeks. Dan was upset to hear the news, especially that he hadn't been considered for that position himself (even though he wasn't ready for it). He worried about it for weeks and began to feel that his company didn't value him and even that his own job might be in jeopardy. His short temper, impatience, and overall negativity began to put a strain on his relationship with his wife and two teenage children. Dan's life, in his mind, was falling apart and, clearly, he was losing control and not coping with the situation very well.

In fact, what actually happened after the four weeks was that the new manager, who was very experienced and highly qualified for the job, came from an organization that was a leader in the industry and had invested heavily in the growth of its staff and management teams. On his first day, the new manger held one-on-one sessions with every member of the team. After he spent two full hours with Dan, asking him about his ideas for improving the department and listening attentively to everything that Dan said, Dan felt much more at ease. Within two months, it was evident to Dan that the change was a positive one, not only for the company, but also for him personally. Unfortunately, Dan had wasted at least four weeks of his life unnecessarily stressed and in fear.

Another characteristic of people who live in the *horizontal* dimension is a feeling that "something is always missing" in their lives and that the present moment, situation, relationship, job, is not good enough. This feeling compels them to spend their time waiting for "something better" to come along, whether this is the weekend, the next holiday, the new car, the new house, the new baby, the new relationship, the new …

Since *now* is not good enough, people who are more horizontally inclined become very attached to their past and the future, as though their life existed only in these two time zones. That perspective stifles growth and creates unnecessary fear and stress—both of which impact negatively on the ability to make progress and move forward. When we look ahead constantly, waiting for a "better" future, we avoid taking chances now, even when, logically, we can see the value of taking a calculated risk for something better. This inner conflict of always wanting something else, and at the same time being too fearful to do what is required to get it, leads to cognitive and emotional dissonance and results in unhappiness and discontent.

Living life horizontally often means doing a lot and keeping busy, but it is mostly busy doing the same types of things *that don't get us any further in life.* Feelings of *dissatisfaction* keep people with a horizontal mind-set on a treadmill, in a place that is ultimately *never* fulfilling. The more we stay horizontal, the heavier we seem to feel and the more complex, or even overwhelming, life seems to be.

The Vertical Perspective

People who are more *vertical* have a clear purpose. At the foundation of this perspective is an orientation toward moving forward. *Vertical* people live a life in which they are constantly charting new territory and creating something new. Living with curiosity and the desire to learn and to experience is vertical living.

Being vertical means living life in the here and now, moment-by-moment, being fully engaged and welcoming change and new opportunities. Vertical people understand that the past is to learn from and that a plan for the future is important for direction and guidance. But the only time in which life can be experienced is in this present moment—the *now*.

Being vertical is also being humble and open to new situations. From a vertical perspective, we look at a situation with new eyes each time it arises and decide how to respond to it in a way that contributes to those who will be affected by that decision. There is no prejudgment—neither positive nor negative—of what a particular situation means, since we understand that each case is a newly arising situation occurring at a specific time and place. All we are required to do is look at it openly and, from that place of openness, respond.

Living vertically means that we see things as constantly new and are enlivened by that reality. If there is anything that we look forward to, it is the emergence and unfolding of life and its progressive nature.

**The horizontal weighs you down;
the vertical allows you to be free.**

The more vertical we are, the lighter we feel and the simpler life seems to be. Vertical living is about giving fully of who you are in every moment and every situation. It is a choice to be *alive* and brings with it an experience of liberation and freedom.

What Are You Choosing?

How much of your day-to-day life do you live vertically, moving forward, fully engaged, and contributing to others—and how much of your day do you live horizontally, feeling that something is missing in your life, waiting for that next thing?

The external situations and events in any day are often the same for vertical and horizontal people, but their internal experiences will be completely different because they are looking at life from a different perspective.

Let's look at an example.

Just as you are leaving the house for work, you look at your watch and realize that you need to hurry if you are to get to work on time for that important 8:00 AM strategy meeting. As you near the bridge, you realize that the traffic is moving extremely slowly. You turn on the radio to listen to the traffic report, but it doesn't explain much. There is a stalled car in your lane, but you are so closely packed that it is difficult to get into the next lane. It is getting closer and closer to your meeting time, and you don't have the cell numbers of the people attending the meeting, and no one can be reached at the office at that time of day. The cars in the next lane also stop. The traffic is jammed. You wait. The traffic starts moving really slowly again. Finally, you get to work, half an hour late for your important meeting.

Let's see how the same event could be experienced very differently from these two perspectives.

From the horizontal perspective, this kind of start to the day would be a real challenge. It would appear that nothing is going according to plan. It feels to you like everyone and everything is getting in your way and preventing you from getting to a very important meeting on time. Your stress level increases, as you realize just how tied up the traffic is, and you can feel the adrenalin start to rush through your body. Your frustration causes you to feel anxious and angry. You wish that the situation could be different. Sitting in the traffic is almost too much to bear, knowing that you are going to be late. You feel helpless and enormously agitated. You wonder, *Why is this happening to me?*

Even for someone living from the vertical perspective, this kind of morning would be challenging. Verticality does not mean that we are untouched by events and external situations. However, you are more likely to accept that you have no control over the traffic and just focus on finding the best possible solution, without wasting your energy on getting stressed or angry. Being caught in the traffic would also not be your first choice, but after realizing that there is nothing more that you can do about the situation other than making the most of it, you accept that you have to wait and find another way to use that time more effectively, such as listening to music, planning the rest of your day, or taking the time to consider a problem that you had been working on for some time. From a vertical perspective, you are aware that this sort of situation can very easily degenerate into frustration and anger, and, therefore, you consciously do something that would lead to a more positive outcome.

Clearly, you would much rather have arrived at the meeting on time, but you understand that there wasn't much you could do to prevent these circumstances. Once you do arrive, although you are still late, you focus on being present and engaged for the rest of the meeting and ensure that you get briefed on what you missed.

With all these unplanned and potentially stressful events taking place, your response from the vertical perspective would in all likelihood be, "Phew, what a start to the day!" But because of your big picture view of the situation, you would then move forward positively instead of dragging an angry and frustrated attitude around all day. When you choose to come from the vertical perspective, you focus on creating new opportunities and constantly improving whatever it is that you are doing. You do this by being clear on what is most important and by being committed to moving forward rather than allowing yourself to get distracted by events over which you have no control.

You are a powerful creator of your own destiny.

Connecting the Dots

Activating your power is a journey or process that requires that you ask yourself three vital questions right up front and again, repeatedly, throughout your journey:

1. Who am I?

2. What am I doing?

3. Why am I doing it?

1. Who am I? This question requires careful contemplation because it provokes us to dig deep within ourselves to gain greater clarity about our purpose, our values, our morals, and our ultimate relationship to life. It requires constant revisiting.

2. What am I doing? This question focuses attention on our behavior and actions, and allows us to determine if we are being true to our highest purpose. It requires serious consideration in everything that we do so that we align ourselves in every moment to what is truly important.

3. Why am I doing it? This question compels us to question our motives in every thought that we have, in every action that we take. This question allows us to discern what is coming from the authentic part of us versus the small, egocentric part of us. We are then free to choose based on our motivation. Each instant becomes a defining moment, which then further clarifies who we really are.

There are other important questions that we can add to these three: *What do I want? Why do I want it? How do I get it? What are the obstacles that are preventing me from getting it?*

Identifying Your Obstacles

Identifying obstacles can be a valuable exercise for helping you to gain more clarity and figure out how to achieve what you want. Perhaps you might come to the conclusion that you are living in the wrong place and need to move to another town or city. Perhaps some parts of your relationship are not working very well, and you need to make some changes. Perhaps your way forward is blocked by a shortage of money, and you need to put together a plan to overcome that. Perhaps you lack educational qualifications and need to further your studies.

Knowing where we tend to get stuck makes it easier to identify the steps to take toward becoming unstuck. A major attitude shift is needed to initiate a total change in the way we live our lives.

Can you see that once you identify what your problems and obstacles are, you have taken the first step toward finding the solutions? Just being able to recognize when you are living horizontally gives you a choice. If you decide to be more vertical, you are ready to move forward in your quest to activate your power.

> *Where there is no vision, the people perish.*
> *—Proverbs 29:18*

Chapter 2

Design a Meaningful Life

Let's imagine that your body is a vehicle, and each day you are driving along on Earth on your life's journey. But where are you headed? Without a destination—a goal or purpose—you won't really get anywhere; you might just wander round in endless circles. You will waste your energy and become increasingly lost, confused, and frustrated.

Finding Your Purpose

The writer and philosopher Henry David Thoreau said, "Most men lead lives of quiet desperation and go to the grave with the song still in them." What a tragically true observation. My own research into human behavior and peak performance led me to conclude that people who are stuck, who believe that they are not living meaningful lives, have this in common: they lack purpose, meaning, and clarity. Even if they do have clarity about where they are going, they are usually not committed enough to their purpose. They are coming from the *horizontal* perspective and, therefore, don't experience much progress. They may wonder if there is a better way to live their lives, but they can't seem to find that way or to make the time to look for it. So, they do what is expected of them and get on with a purposeless life, operating in survival mode. They work in jobs that often don't inspire them and are involved in relationships that are not fulfilling. From time to time, the voice returns to haunt them: *Is this all there is?* They dismiss it and continue on the same path.

In order to live a successful and meaningful life, conscious effort is required to design that life. Designing your life begins with finding and committing to your highest purpose. We all have a purpose in life. It may be consciously or only unconsciously known to us, but it is the driving force behind every action that we take and the consequences that arise from these actions.

I want a purpose that is inspiring to me, one that will compel me to jump out of bed every morning for the right reasons not the wrong ones. I want it to be a purpose that stimulates me to be engaged with what I do and with whom I am, and one that makes the most of what I am good at or have the potential to be good at.

Once you identify what your purpose is, you will know without a shadow of a doubt that it is what you are meant to be doing. Life then takes on a whole new meaning, and you begin to feel liberated and inspired, as though you have been given a new lease on life.

> *The meaning of life is to find your gift.*
> *The purpose of life is to share that gift.*
> —Joy J. Golliver

Is It Too Late to Start?

How do we ensure that we find our true purpose and express our "song" rather than take it to the grave with us? What if we are halfway or more through our lives—is it too late to begin?

I recently saw the movie *Away from Her,* about a woman afflicted with Alzheimer's disease and her husband who was caring for her. One of the lines in the movie was, "It's never too late to become what you might have been." It is a powerful statement. It is never too late to find and live your true purpose.

Defining Your Purpose

So then, what is your *highest* purpose? In other words, what is the main reason why you get out of bed every morning? This may be the most difficult, and at the same time most important, question that you can ask yourself. And since this question has been the cornerstone of most philosophies, and ultimately lies in the realms of emotion and spirituality, many people don't know where or how to begin seeking the answer.

You may find the question easier to tackle if you break it down into components, asking instead:

- What were the most special experiences of my life, when I felt completely absorbed and time just flew by?
- What activities make me feel really good about myself?
- Which activities or experiences fill me with extreme happiness and gratitude?
- What makes, or would make, me feel passionate and more alive?
- How can I bring more meaning into my life?
- Which career would be the most inspirational to me, or how could I find inspiration in the job I am doing?

Identify Your Core Values

❖ Try this simple exercise to direct your thoughts toward identifying your purpose in life. Thinking of your own core values, ask yourself: *What is most important in my life?* Write down everything that comes to mind, even if you have 156 items on your list. Next, rank them in order of importance.

You will find that when you identify your true core values, you will have an emotional reaction to what you wrote. That is one way of directing yourself toward your purpose: "listening" to your reaction to the items on your list. Remember that your purpose will include *all* the things that are important to you. My own purpose may include raising mentally, emotionally, and physically healthy children, but since making a difference in the lives of other people is another core value for me, it also needs to be part of my purpose.

When you have discovered what matters most to you, it becomes easier to find your purpose. When you find or create your purpose, you know that you are living as you should be and doing what you should be doing. You feel motivated, fulfilled, and excited as you make a difference in your own and others' lives. You obtain a sense of fulfillment and connection to your core values.

Some people know what their purpose is when they are very young. Most of us are not that fortunate. For me, my purpose suddenly became very clear to me when I had my wake-up call. I realized that in order to live a happy and fulfilled life, I needed to feel that I was contributing to others rather than focusing only on myself.

Now when I ask myself the questions above, my answers still center around my family, working with people whom I enjoy, and finding creative solutions for improving performance and quality of life. Some of the most important values in my life include the nurturing of close relationships, creativity, promoting growth and development, and meaningful exploration. When I am doing activities that are aligned to my purpose, I feel happy and alive and know that this is what I am meant to be doing.

❖ I suggest you take the time to write down a sentence or two that defines your purpose as you see it for yourself right now. This sentence, or sentences, can evolve with time or as you gain further insights. I have mine typed into my phone, and I find it very useful to refer to it whenever I am not sure how to proceed, or even just as a daily reminder of the direction I wish to take with my life.

Let your purpose be your guide.

Maintaining the Focus

When we live our lives in alignment to our purpose, to our core values, to what is most important to us, we find that we enjoy ourselves more, we feel true and honorable, we are more creative, happier, and able to make a difference. It is that simple. So why is it that more people are not living their purpose? What is preventing them?

I am sure that once you have discovered or defined your own purpose, you will hear many "voices" telling you why you don't have what it takes to live according to that purpose. These voices can come from outside (from others) or from inside your own head, but either way, they usually result in procrastination and inaction. For example, when I decided that I wanted to live my purpose, it involved changing from a regular job to starting my own business, something I had never done before. My inner voices came up with many reasons for not following through with it: the possibility of failure, unnecessary risk, embarrassment, losing face, and many others. Fortunately, my inspiration and commitment to living my newfound purpose was stronger than the trap of my ego's negative thoughts and self-doubt. I didn't listen to the voices but, rather, did what my deepest feelings compelled me to do—be true to what I believed. I realized that I am responsible for deciding what my purpose is and that I owe it to myself to live *my* life in the best way that I possibly can. Identifying your purpose is something that you do on your own, acknowledging your own core values, regardless of what anyone else may think.

Being very clear about the nature of your purpose, as well as fully committed to it, ensures that all your effort and activity is directed toward achieving it. When the question, *What is life all about?* comes to mind, the answer should be very clear to you. If there is lack of clarity, your energy will be scattered and, therefore, wasted. Once you are fully clear and committed to your purpose, you will no longer question why you have to get out of bed every morning. Nor will you wonder what point there is in doing whatever it is that you are doing, or in being with whomever you are with. In fact, after you have identified your purpose in life, it is very difficult to keep living a meaningless and uninspired life. As Helen Keller once said, "One can never consent to creep when one feels an impulse to soar."

Living your purpose also requires altering your lifestyle. It does not necessarily mean that you have to erase your current life, as Mother Theresa did at the age of eighteen, when she decided to devote her life to religion and walked away from her family, never to see them again. But you can use what you have discovered about yourself to make your current path (personal and career) more meaningful. When you are clear on your purpose, it becomes easier to walk away from those activities, people, or things that distract you from, or do not contribute to, that purpose. When you are fully committed to your purpose, you no longer dissipate your energy and allow distractions to control your life. When you seriously commit to your purpose, you free yourself from fear, insecurity, and doubt and experience a feeling of connection.

As you progress through this book, it will become clear that your purpose encompasses everything in your life. In fact, not only does it touch on every important aspect of your life, but it also influences the lives of those around you.

Using Your Purpose to Design Your Life

Believe it or not, many people do not have total control over what they think and how they feel. On the contrary, they allow much of their lives to be governed by external influences: by world events and specific local situations; by the media; by what other people say, think, and do; or by circumstances in general, often referred to as "fate." When people allow external factors—the weather, the traffic, their boss, or a family member—to affect the way they feel or behave, they are overly vulnerable to influences over which they have little or no control. Small wonder that they have so much stress in their lives. External events and situations and people control their lives, leaving them feeling powerless and anxious.

There is a solution. As we will see as we proceed through the following chapters, by activating your power and following your highest purpose, you can change your current vulnerability and reactive way of behaving (that is, reacting to external events and circumstances) and realize instead that you can have control over your own thoughts and feelings. You can gain immense power by understanding that your thoughts are energy manifested into reality and that you are like quantum magnets (see chapter 4), attracting "like" energy to yourself.

***When you fully commit to your purpose,
your energy becomes focused and powerful.***

When you decide to make your purpose the primary driver in your life, you will discover courage, strength, and laser-like focus that you did not know you had. You will have access to an inner confidence and peace that can only be realized when fear is no longer the master ruling your life.

Purpose and Perspective

Your ability to follow the purpose you have identified for yourself is undeniably affected by your overall perspective, and here I mean the perspectives we introduced in chapter 1: *horizontal* and *vertical*. It is, therefore, important that we have a thorough understanding of these perspectives and their degrees.

The "Normal" Horizontal Perspective

Take a look at figure 1A and imagine that the dotted line represents your life path. The middle horizontal block represents the place where the majority of people operate most of the time. We'll call this place the *normal horizontal level*.

A horizontal life, as we have seen, is primarily concerned with survival and coping. The main question that people at this level ask is, *"How can I cope better?"* People here are predominantly on autopilot for a large part of their lives. Like leaves drifting in a stream, they allow their lives to be mostly buffeted by external forces.

People's actions at this level are *reactive*, often automatic, and mainly based on triggers (stimuli) from outside influences. When we are at this level, we might realize we are not fully in control, but mostly we feel we are powerless to do anything about it. Some days we are up, and some days we are down. We just float through our days on the current of the river of life … up, down, up, down, up, down, helplessly swept along. When we are down, we work very hard to get back up again, and like corks forced underwater, we do naturally tend to bob up to the surface.

But at this level, being up is usually only temporary. We may feel good, confident, and happy, but only until the next negative event or situation prompts us to go down again. Very often, even when we are up and everything seems to be so good, a little voice comes along and says, *Life is too good for me right now, and I know that it's only a matter of time before something is going to happen and I go down again.* And of course, something *does* happen, and the cycle continues.

Horizontal happiness is only temporary.

At the normal horizontal level, most people operate out of *fear* and *craving*. These two forces drive many things: people's thoughts, actions, and emotions, even the stock exchange. Share prices are elevated by people buying shares that they believe will make them

Figure 1A

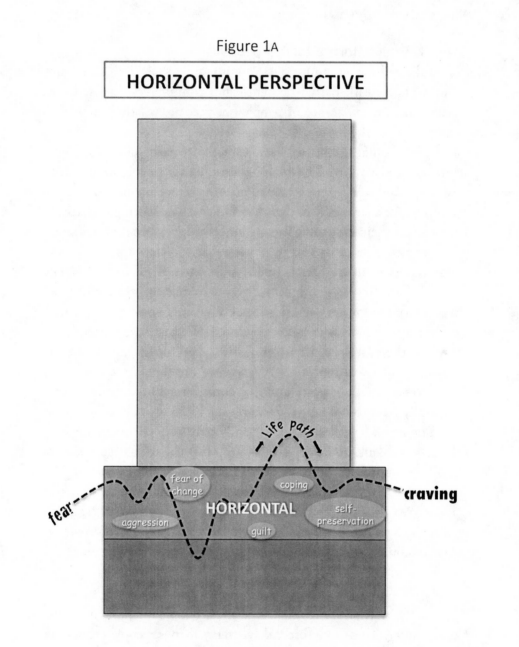

rich (craving), and the prices fall when people sell shares to avoid losing money (fear). When we are at the horizontal level, we are driven by the fear of losing things (our relationships, jobs, material possessions, status, reputation, and respect) and by cravings for the same things (better relationships and jobs, better cars, bigger houses, more money, higher status, greater respect).

Fear

How does fear operate in most people's lives? Millions of people get out of bed each day and go to work not because they find their work meaningful or even enjoyable but because they fear that if they don't go to work, they won't get paid. If they don't get paid, they won't be able to provide for their families and themselves. If they can't meet their families' essential needs, they feel they will have failed in the most basic way and may even be rejected by those they love the most.

Many people's lives are fear based, full of worries such as: *What if I don't perform at the levels that I have been until now? What will my family/friends/colleagues say? What if he/she finds someone much better than I? What if I end up finding nobody and have to spend the rest of my life alone?*

I experienced a tremendous "aha" moment once during a casual conversation I had with one of my clients many years ago.

This client was the chairman of a group of highly successful companies that operated across many different industries. He was regarded as extremely successful by any business measurement and had "made it" financially. I was amazed by his talent and business acumen and leadership, and I was also very curious to find out what was driving him to work at the extreme pace that he still kept. So, one day I asked him that question. We were sitting together in a cab on the way to the airport, when I told him that ever since I started working with his various organizations, I had been curious about what drives a highly successful entrepreneur like him to continue to give his life and soul to the business. He paused for a few seconds and then replied with an answer that astounded me: "My key driving motivator and what keeps me working like I do," he said, "is the fear of failure."

The biggest insight I obtained from his admission was that fear is a much bigger motivator than most people would like to believe, and that although being driven by fear can lead to external and material success, the price is an incessant and nagging pain that diminishes our happiness and quality of life.

In part 2 of this book, we look at strategies for achieving incredible success without having to be driven by fear or external motivators.

Craving: Have-Do-Be

The flip side of fear, craving (or the desire for more), is an equal motivator at the normal horizontal level. People at this level subscribe to the *Have-Do-Be* formula. This is how it works:

*When I **have** (more money, better friends, a better job, a better relationship), then I will **do** what I really want to do (move to another place, start my own business, tour the world), and then I will **be** happier, more successful, and more fulfilled.*

Does that sound familiar?

The biggest drawback to this formula is that it sets us up to wait perpetually for better conditions. When people subscribe to the *Have-Do-Be* formula, their feelings and acknowledgment of happiness and success are put on hold while they wait endlessly for that winning ticket or ideal job, that satisfying situation, or that perfect relationship before they can declare themselves truly satisfied and successful.

At all levels of society, we can find people who are constantly looking for something more. *I want more of this and more of that. I don't have enough. I need more. More of this, and more of that…* Almost everyone wants more, and there's nothing wrong with having more. What is important, though, is to explore what your true motivation for *wanting* really is. Is it driven by fear and craving, or is the wanting more aligned with your higher values and principles, your purpose?

Craving: Do-Have-Be

There is another group of people who operate at the normal horizontal level and, by most standards, are often regarded as the successful people in our society. They use a slightly more progressive model called the *Do-Have-Be* formula, which works like this:

*I will **do** this, and then I will **have** that, and then I will **be** happy, more successful, and more fulfilled.*

This model is more productive than the first one because it prompts action, and when the right action is taken, results are ultimately achieved. But despite the results that people obtain with this formula, it still holds a trap into which many people in our society fall. The trap is that they are on the endless treadmill of having to *do* something in order to *have* something in order to *be* something.

There is a very strong compulsion at the normal horizontal level to feel like a *somebody*. Many of us have been conditioned to want to become somebody based on the Western culture's definition of success—predominately wealth, fame, power, and status. Many "successful" people who fall into this trap find that their wealth, power, fame, and status give them more choices and comfort. But as long as their motivation is still based on fear and craving, the feelings of happiness are only temporary. The inner voice is still lurking in the background, and before long, they are back on the treadmill, feeling that something is still missing, as they work toward the next project that will fulfill them, complete them, and free them.

It really doesn't matter whether you are a junior clerk or the CEO of a large corporation. The point is not *what you have* but *what you do with what you have*. Are you fulfilled, joyful, and free? Are you contributing more to others when you have more yourself? Is your energy directed toward proving yourself to the world to gain greater recognition, attention, and validation, or is it aimed at benefiting others?

Chinese Taoist philosopher Lao Tzu said, *"He who knows he has enough is rich."* Put this way, it seems simple to escape the mind-set that enslaves us with fear and craving. But until we reach that state of contentment, let's see what happens when we allow these forces to drag us down even lower than the normal horizontal level.

The Extreme Horizontal Perspective

Look at figure 1B. You will see that below the normal horizontal level, there is an even lower level. Although most people remain in the normal horizontal zone in their day-to-day lives, there are times when we experience even deeper levels of pain and lack of clarity. We will call this level the "extreme" horizontal level. This is where life is a real struggle, where survival is the single objective. We are not talking about simple physical survival but, rather, survival of the soul.

The extreme horizontal level is where depression is a common companion; it is a kingdom ruled by negativity, pessimism, pain, and fear. It is a place to which people are driven when bad things happen and they cannot cope. Some people drop into the extreme horizontal because of an isolated event in their lives, such as the death of someone close, loss of a job, divorce, or any other event that triggers them to sink to that level. People who are at this level find daily life extremely painful, complex, and heavy. It is very difficult to see things in a positive light from here because life feels dark and out of control.

Not surprisingly, when people see things from the perspective of the extreme horizontal, they feel an overwhelming urge to escape. But because most people do not have the tools to do this in a natural and permanent way, they often turn to artificial means, which may take the form of addiction. They hope that these external crutches will take them out of the desperate place in which they find themselves, and they hold onto their addictions because at some level, they dull the pain. They are driven to seek fulfillment outside of themselves, but no substance or destructive behavior can ever permanently fill the void or heal the emotional wound that they are experiencing.

Addictions begin with pain, and end with more pain.

Even though addictive substances or behaviors (drugs, alcohol, sex, etc.) may provide some short-term relief, in the long term, they only spiral the person deeper and deeper into the depths of despair. The escape is only temporary. Before long, the effects wear off, and people at the extreme horizontal level find that their problems haven't gone away. So they indulge in their addiction again and again. Eventually, they may become completely dependent on these substances or behaviors to numb and suppress their pain and suffering.

Figure 1B

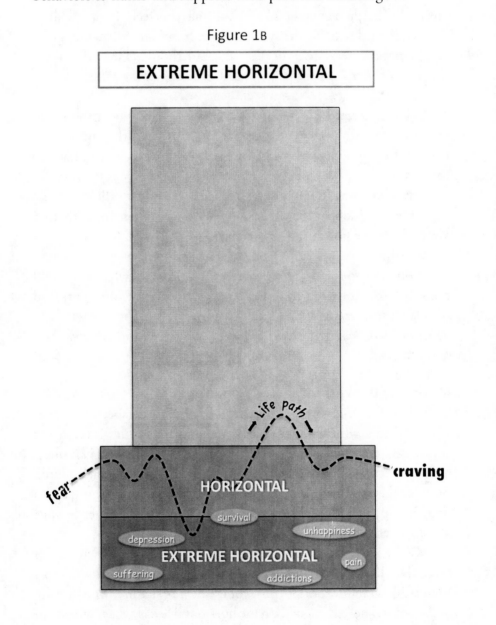

Survival

The controlling force at this extreme horizontal level is profound fear, fear that often turns to panic. There is a single driving thought and instinct—*I need to survive!*

At this level, the survival urge is not only psychological but also physical. The pain may be so intense that you feel physically ill or even close to death. You may experience humiliation, shame, guilt, regret, extreme fear, grief, or despair. Your thoughts may run along the lines of, *I'm not making it. I need to do something drastic because I'm just not coping here.*

Below a certain line, people feel that the situation is hopeless, and, therefore, they move into apathy. At this level, they might lose the will to go on. The cork-like instinct that bounces them back to the surface is just not there anymore.

But what most people don't realize when they fall into these depths is that the solution lies *within*. We need to remember that we always have the power: *the power to choose.*

Each one of us has the power to choose what to do in any situation, how to respond to things, and, ultimately, whether to hold onto them or let them go. You can get all the advice you want, read books, go to therapists, and attend seminars. But nothing will help you until *you make the decision to take charge of your life and start taking action.*

Moving to the Vertical

If you feel that you are currently holding a perspective that is not consistent with who you really are, and that your vision of the future is bigger than the life you are currently living, you can make a choice *right now* to do something about it. In a nutshell, doing more of the same will only get you more of the same. You have to do things differently, act in a way that will move you closer to your goals and aspirations.

We all have the ability to move to a state where we are more vertical, to live a happy and boundless life if we choose to. It is almost impossible to follow our purpose, or create a better life, when we are at the normal horizontal or extreme horizontal levels. The momentum of the driving forces of fear and greed are too overwhelming for most people to overcome and control. It is, therefore, vital to understand that in order to create a better life, we need to change to the vertical perspective.

The Importance of Being Honest with Yourself

It is critically important that we honestly acknowledge not only what is missing in our lives but also the full extent to which we are concerned about ourselves. This self-concern leads to a horizontal perspective in almost everything that we do.

By being honest with ourselves about the pettiness of many aspects of our life, and by juxtaposing that against our deeply felt yearnings to be truly unselfish and to leave the world a better place than we found it, we can be inspired to make the deep effort required to transform ourselves and our lives into something more meaningful.

From Selfishness to Altruism

At the extreme horizontal level, negative energy drains the life force from everyone around us—at home, at work, and in social situations. We are like energy vampires. At this level, the outcome is *Lose-Lose*.

At the next level, the normal horizontal, we are egocentric, self-centered, and often competitive; the mind-set is *as long as I win*. We look at the world primarily from a selfish perspective. Since this also applies to our relationships, we are all too apt to ask, *"How can I get the most out of this relationship?"* Or, similarly, at work, *"How can I get the most out of this job?"*

By contrast, at the vertical levels, a *Win-Win-Win* orientation prevails. At these levels, our main focus is for all concerned, and winning only makes sense if it is a win at all levels—for the individual, as well as for the group, the family, or the organization.

At these levels, *We* supersedes *I*, and our goals become integration, continuous development,

> *Don't ask, 'What is the meaning of life?' but rather, 'What is life asking of me?'*
> —Viktor Frankl

and collaboration. Life here is about growth, thriving on change, and holding dear the purpose of creating a better world.

Figure 1c

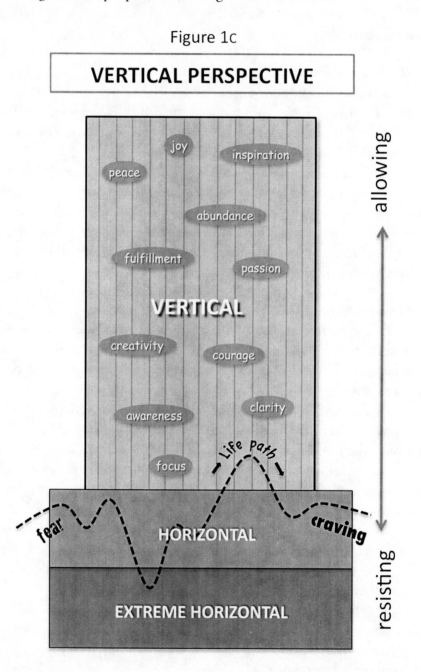

The Vertical Perspective

When we are comfortably placed in the vertical perspective, we experience feelings of inner peace, joy, and contentment (see figure 1C.) These are restful states in which we can sit and rejuvenate ourselves. At the vertical level, we also experience passion, focus, abundance, and courage and are inspired to take positive action.

❖ In order to understand this perspective more deeply, sit quietly and remember a time when you felt fulfilled, free, joyful, and at peace. Relive that experience.

When you are more vertical, you feel awake, aware, and in tune with what is going on around you. You are aware that you are part of everything. You see with greater clarity and feel engaged and connected to life.

Verticality does not mean that life suddenly becomes perfect and positive in every way and at all times. What it does mean is that you are conscious of your moment-by-moment movement through your life so that you become an active participant in it, rather than a spectator who only gets drawn in every now and again. While life is still filled with all kinds of challenges, nothing holds you back from staying conscious and making mindful choices that empower you and help you to move forward.

From the vertical perspective, we feel more connected to life.

It is a little bit like surfing. When you are trying to catch the crest of a wave, initially it is a lot of hard work, but once you reach it, all you do is focus on staying on the edge—a new edge that forms moment by moment. In that place, there is joy, exhilaration, freedom, and excitement. In that moment, you are not thinking of anything else. You are simply present, totally there, focused and in tune with the way life is unfolding.

Freedom to Achieve

Those who are in the horizontal state are constantly distracted and miss a lot of opportunities. They are, therefore, often taken by surprise when something happens, since they were not aware that it was developing. By the time they do see it, they are forced to act quickly and, therefore, often make poor decisions.

If you are more conscious and able to see the situation as it develops, you will have more time and space to consider how you want to respond to it. This removes a lot of the stress from everyday life and creates a greater feeling of freedom.

The vertical perspective allows us to get things done, create new things, and move forward with positive action. This is the perspective from which great artists and musicians have created when we recognize something profound in their work.

At the vertical level, we are not held back by selfishness, fear, greed, doubt, and insecurity. People often refer to our history of emotional wounds as "baggage." I prefer to think of it as a heavy rock that we carry with us wherever we go. This rock can grow larger and heavier over time. When we are truly vertical, we are no longer carrying this heavy rock of our emotional past. When we put down the rock, we experience the relief and lightness that comes with our unburdened state. Unencumbered, we can move forward freely.

Verticality and Happiness

When we are happy, we find that we like others more, we are more patient and interested, and generally treat people in a more caring way. When we are happy, it is unlikely that we will treat others disrespectfully or intentionally set out to hurt their feelings. We feel free and do not feel the need to protect ourselves.

When we are hurt or angry, on the other hand, we become angry and irritated with others much more quickly. Our general feeling of unhappiness colors our world, and nothing looks particularly appealing or beautiful. We hit out to protect ourselves and go around spreading our gloomy energy.

Happy people are infectious. Unfortunately, the opposite is also true: fear breeds fear.

So How Does Your Perspective Affect Your Ability to Design a Meaningful Life?

Your power to create what you want from life is directly affected by your perspective. The more horizontal your perspective, the more difficult it is to achieve results and the longer it takes. The more vertical your perspective, the faster you can create the life that you truly want, and with much greater ease.

Creating a meaningful life can be likened to growing plants in a garden. At the extreme horizontal level, the garden is filled with weeds the size of trees. These massive weeds suck all of the nutrients from the soil, leaving the dreams that you want to cultivate without fertilizer or room to grow.

The normal horizontal level is significantly better. Some of what you plant is able to survive and slowly begins to bear fruit, but since there are still a lot of weeds demanding your energy and attention, you are not able to accomplish anything close to your full potential. Much of what you plant does not grow, and that which does grows slowly and sparsely.

At the vertical level, there are very few, if any, weeds at all. The soil is healthy and fertile. Seeds that you plant have the potential to blossom almost instantly, and your ability to create is far beyond what most people believe is possible.

What Do You Really Want in Life?

Let's take a whole new look at what you really want in life. Look at the perspective model and ask yourself the following question: *What do I really want in my life that will reflect who I really am?*

If you decide that you want to be seriously committed to creating a better future for yourself, your family, and those around you, you are ready to activate your power.

As soon as you make the choice to view your life in this way, a significant shift takes place because you have decided to become a full participant in the creative process of life. You become more resourceful and feel more powerful; you have more energy throughout the day, at work, and at home. You are at ease and begin to experience a state of "flow," where things happen without effort, as though some higher power is working through you and with you.

This energy is so powerful, so exhilarating, and so satisfying that it enables you to create positive and profound changes in your world and the larger world around you.

The Biggest Challenge Is at Liftoff

Imagine a rocket that is about to take off from Earth to space. In the entire journey, when will the most energy be needed? Right at the beginning, at liftoff. It takes an enormous amount of energy to overcome the inertia of standing still; the powerful pull of gravity holds it firmly to the ground. As the rocket progresses on its journey, however, things become easier and easier, and when it finally reaches orbit, it is mostly propelled by its own momentum.

> *Cherish your visions and your dreams, as they are the children of your soul; the blueprints of your ultimate achievements.*
> — *Napoleon Hill*

Making a change in life presents a similar challenge. The most difficult part is often overcoming inertia and getting started. Getting beyond this point requires a great deal of effort, focus, and commitment. You have to be serious about your journey because you are sure to encounter many obstacles along the way. But as you progress on your path, it becomes easier and easier, until it takes very little energy to continue.

The most difficult part is overcoming the inertia and getting started.

One of the biggest obstacles to personal change is the tendency for society to want to pull us back toward the norm. When we try to step outside it, we often experience negative reactions from the people around us. That is because most of society is at the horizontal level, and they will do everything to try to keep us there with them—not for our sake, but for *their* sake—because of fear and insecurity.

Chapter 3

Understand Your Biggest Obstacle

Welcome to the Ego!

What is it that keeps so many people from moving to the vertical perspective? Surely we all wish to live a more vertical life. So is there something keeping us in the horizontal? There is, in fact, a powerful counter force to our desire to take off, something most people have heard about but few fully understand. Welcome to your ego.

The ego is best described as the inauthentic, false self. It is who we think we are, that part of us that we identify with most closely. The ego part in each of us arises at a very young age for the main purpose of protecting us from external threats and potential harm. Unchecked, it becomes a dominating force that strives to control every aspect of our lives (events, people, and situations), compete with others, and separate from others to preserve its own identity. The ego is our constant companion at the horizontal levels, talking to us persistently in our own voice and making it difficult for us to know whether we are hearing our ego or our real selves. We can easily become slaves to our egos, even though they lead to negative feelings of fear, insecurity, and self-doubt. These fears trap us in the ego, as they manifest in us as both passive and defensive behaviors that prevent us from making decisions from a more vertical perspective.

The ego only has the ability to use past experience and project that into the future, and thus, it often acts in error. Living through our ego means, then, that we are not fully aware of everything that is happening right now, in the present. Instead, we constantly recall what happened before and then react based on the past. When we live our lives through the ego, we are stuck in the horizontal dimension and are not able to see the full truth of what is happening in this moment.

Beware: your ego talks to you in your own voice!

The Ego Illustrated

As an example from my own experience, shortly after my promotion to first line manager at Unilever many years ago, I was asked to deliver a presentation to the senior leadership team. Although I knew the content well, I was petrified about my delivery, about what they would think of me if the presentation were not interesting and engaging. I spent the three weeks leading up to that presentation worrying about my image, my future in the company, and whether I even had what it takes to be a manager—all of which caused me to have many sleepless nights. I eventually delivered the presentation successfully, but the self-inflicted ordeal that I went through beforehand drained a large part of my energy and my ability to be effective for several weeks.

Why was I feeling that way? Why such an enormous reaction to, really, such a small task? What was it that made me so scared and insecure? Was public speaking or presenting really the issue? I was worried that people would question my ability and competence, which would ultimately lead to a negative outcome. But from where did these feelings of inadequacy come?

It was only later in my life that I realized that presenting in front of a group was not my real fear. Rather, my ego was projecting from an incident that occurred when I was in the eighth grade, causing turmoil every time there was a chance that I might reexperience the emotional trauma of my thirteen-year-old self.

Every student in my eighth grade class had been given the task of presenting an English essay in front of the whole class. I didn't prepare properly, and when my turn came, my presentation was poor. I felt humiliated and projected these feelings onto the way I thought others felt about me. That experience created an "emotional wound" in my subconscious mind, causing me to believe at a young age that I wasn't good enough.

My ego never forgot that incident (but reinforced it with similar experiences throughout my life), and each time there was a threat to my self-image, it would react by causing stress in the hope that I would not take the risk. In a way, my ego convinced me that it was protecting me from being hurt again. It was only when I finally decided that I wanted to move forward in my life that I recognized the need to step outside of my comfort zone, or the prison that the ego had created for me (with my unconscious consent), and into a new world of possibilities.

Understand Your Ego

When we are blinded by the workings of the ego and don't see it for what it is, our fears often prevent us from doing what we really want to do, or from being who we really want to be. And, therefore, our lives become characterized by dissatisfaction, feelings of lack (something is always missing), and constant waiting for more, better, and/or bigger! This is why so many people get stressed, frustrated, and often disappointed, irrespective of how good their life situations are.

The ego acts like a cloud cover that prevents us from seeing the full extent of the sun (the light). Recognizing your ego is like recovering from partial blindness. It reminds me of the famous song "Amazing Grace," written about the abolition of the British Empire's slave trade. The words, "I once was lost but now am found, was blind but now I see," can also refer to the abolishment of the ego and the ability to "see the light," or, in other words, the truth of who we really are.

Understanding how the ego works in your everyday life allows you to better understand yourself. When you recognize that the ego is just *one part* of your individual identity, not the whole, it is easier to regain the power to choose more vertically (or authentically) rather than making choices that are self-centered and horizontal.

Let's look at some of the characteristics of the ego obstacle and examine how it operates.

Characteristics of the Ego

We need to understand the ego's characteristics in order to be able to distinguish between what is ego and what is real. Many people think that the ego is primarily arrogance, but on further analysis, we observe that the ego permeates many parts of our lives in devious and cunning ways. It is important to note that it is always the same ego; it just changes masks to avoid detection and, thereby, continues to protect itself.

1. Self-Protection

The essential characteristic of the ego is that it will do anything and everything to survive. Its self-protective instincts are awesomely powerful, and its primary task is ensuring that the *me* is kept guarded and safe from hurt or the reopening of an emotional wound.

Inherent in all of us is a strong yearning to be deeply connected to others; yet the ego's manipulative strategies are geared toward maintaining our "little secrets" or the selfish motive of protecting "me." Ironically, in order to keep the me safe, the ego

> *What a liberation to realize that the "voice in my head" is not who I am. Who am I then? The one who sees that.*
> —Eckhart Tolle

works to our detriment by creating a sense of separation from others through a complex defense structure. The ego constantly reminds us of events in which we were betrayed or taken advantage of by people to whom we were close. "No more!" says the ego. "Once bitten, twice shy. I am not going to fall for that again. I will no longer allow myself to experience these feelings of shame, regret, inadequacy, and pain. Even in intimate relationships, I will keep a part of me only to myself so that I can stay safe and protected."

So the ego induces competitiveness, controlling and oppositional behaviors, lack of trust, fear (of rejection, humiliation, or inadequacy), approval seeking, and sometimes even aggression. We react to the ego's warnings by protecting ourselves and ensuring that we are safe from anything we perceive as a potential threat, whether it be change, other people, work colleagues, or sometimes even our own family members. In this light, it is easy to understand why so many people find it difficult to sustain deep and intimate relationships.

2. Resistance to Change

One of the biggest triggers for the ego is *change,* because change, in most cases, means uncertainty, and uncertainty suggests that we will no longer be able to control our future. This threatens the ego, which needs to feel that it's in constant control of everything. The fear that we experience in the face of change causes us to contract and guard against this external threat, even when we believe that making the change will lead to positive outcomes. The ego is not driven by logic but rather by emotions stimulated by irrational and nonsensical projections.

Can you remember times in your life when you resisted—even strongly resisted—change, only to realize later that it would have been for the better? Perhaps you had a dream about which you felt very inspired. One part of you was very excited about the new possibility, but unfortunately, there was another part that was fearful and full of doubt and uncertainty over what would happen and whether you would succeed or fail. So, in the end, you let that dream go.

These kinds of situations are typically experienced as the *divided self,* which is ego. The authentic, or vertical, part of us wants to create and is excited about moving forward. But the ego slows us by generating negative emotions that become obstacles we have to overcome. This struggle consumes a lot of energy that could be better utilized.

3. Self-Doubt

The ego's fear of change is fueled by our self-doubt and insecurities. This is the reason people who are more horizontal tend to be unable to take a leap into unknown and potentially risky territories.

A friend of mine (I'll call her Cathy) told me a story of what happened to her when she was fourteen. She was the highest ranked tennis player at her tennis club for her age group that year, and her dream was to be a great tennis player. She played often and won often; her confidence was high, and she enjoyed the game very much. One day, she was told that she would be playing a new member at the club who was a very good and talented player. Cathy looked forward to the game but was beaten in three straight sets. The game was grueling, and she was totally outplayed in every conceivable way. Cathy was humbled by a great tennis player, and her belief in her ability to be a notable player herself one day instantly vanished into thin air. She fell into the ego's trap of self-doubt, and within two weeks of that embarrassing defeat, she quit tennis. What a shame! What a waste!

❖ Take a moment to recall some of the self-doubt and insecurities that have influenced major choices in your life. What might your life have been like had you not fallen into these traps of self-doubt? Finally, ask yourself, *In which areas do I currently feel insecure and self-doubting and what can I do to ensure that I don't fall into the ego trap again?*

Now that you have recognized these limiting doubts, you can make the appropriate choices that will overcome these barriers. Your ego does not have to impede your future decisions and actions.

4. General Fear

When you were a young child, you may have been afraid of monsters in the dark. Now that you are an adult, you know that such monsters are not real—don't you? Or is it simply the nature of those imaginary monsters that has changed, and you still behave as if they were real?

Most of our fears are illusory, but when our ego is engaged, our mental, emotional, and physical experiences make these fears seem real. An acronym that can help us remember what FEAR really means is, *false evidence appearing real*. In other words, many of our fears and causes of anxiety appear much bigger and far more real than they actually are.

Stress management experts say that only 2 percent of our "worrying time" is spent on things that might actually be helped by worrying. The figures below illustrate how the other 98 percent of this time is spent:

- 40 percent on things that never happen
- 35 percent on things that can't be changed

- 15 percent on things that turn out better than expected
- 8 percent on useless, petty worries

So, 98 percent of the time, our worrying doesn't accomplish anything, yet we continually worry. We worry about our finances, our homes, our possessions. We worry about our children, our parents, our health, and our future.

Ninety-eight percent of our worries never materialize.

When people fall into the ego's trap of fear, they become worried and anxious about something in the future that will likely never happen. I often see this occur when organizations restructure and there is uncertainty about the future. Staff members, at all levels, who do not have sufficient information about the changes and their potential impact begin to speculate on what will happen, who it will happen to, and how it will happen. They often predict the worst-case scenario, which means doom and gloom, and feel that their own position, status, or job is at stake. Corporate politics and lobbying begin to escalate, and before long, people stop focusing on their work and become unproductive, spending a large part of their time and energy worrying and waiting to see what happens. So much energy is wasted! Then, after the initial shock and uncertainty, people eventually settle back into their existing or new roles … until the next restructure, merger, or acquisition starts a whole new cycle of fear, uncertainty, and anxiety. At some level, most people fear that it's only a matter of time before something else happens and starts the whole cycle again.

You may argue that some fear is necessary to keep you safe from real danger. Although your ego would like to convince you of that, it's generally not true. It is important to make a distinction between fear and common sense: the reason we don't cross the road during peak-hour traffic is not because we fear the road or, for that matter, cars. The reason we don't do it is because *common sense* tells us that if we did, our life would be in danger or we may get severely injured. It is our common sense that protects us and keeps us safe, not the overpowering feelings of fear, as is often believed. Most of our fears are not helpful but simply limiting.

❖ I recommend that every six months you do the "Face My Fears" exercise, which consists of four steps:

Step 1:   Make a list of your three greatest fears.

Step 2:   Develop a plan to overcome each one of these fears. Make sure that the plan is sensible and rational rather than impulsive and that it takes into consideration those who may be impacted by it.

Step 3:   Take action and face those fears.

Step 4:   Be aware of how your self-confidence and feelings of empowerment increase as you face more and more of your fears.

5. Superiority or Inferiority

Another manifestation of ego is a feeling of superiority. Your ego may act with pride and demand that you be seen as all-knowing. It fills you with righteous indignation and convinces you that you are always right. Instead of being open, flexible, and receptive to new ideas and ways of doing things, your ego causes you to be relatively closed and inflexible.

The flip side of this characteristic is inferiority. The playground or corporate bully behaves with what seems to be arrogance and superiority, while deep inside, these behaviors stem from feelings of inferiority and inadequacy. Perhaps you suspect that you can never do anything right and constantly put yourself down. It may seem strange that the ego will pose as inferior, but remember that acting weak is just another form of self-protection through manipulation. People who feel inferior may seek the approval of others for protection or ensure that they don't do anything that may expose the pain of their emotional wound to others. I am sure that you know people who manipulate by acting inferior and insecure around others, thereby triggering feelings of guilt, which, in turn, lead to overcompensation and often dysfunctional relationships.

6. Justification

When your ego is in the driver's seat, it finds plenty of justification for why you don't have to change or do anything that may expose you. We all are very familiar with blaming a situation, circumstance, or even someone else so that we don't have to take responsibility ourselves.

❖ Stop for a moment and recall a situation that you were in recently where you may have thought, for example, *I can't confront X with this now because of Y, or Z MADE me do it, which caused @#!*

I remember when I emigrated to Canada and decided to start my own business in my new country. I began to interview local businesses to find out what the culture was in Canada, and British Columbia in particular, what the needs of these local organizations were, and also whether what I had to offer would be suitable for that market. Within a very short space of time, I began

> *Each man has only one genuine vocation—to find himself. His task is to discover his own destiny— not an arbitrary one—and live it out wholly and resolutely, within himself. Everything else is only a would-be existence, an attempt at evasion, a flight back to the ideals of the masses, conformity, and fear of one's own inwardness.*
> —Herman Hesse

to realize that the Canadian culture—more specifically, the culture in British Columbia—was somewhat different to what I was used to in Johannesburg, South Africa. I was used to fast decisions and quick action, but now, in this new culture, I needed to slow down.

Initially, this wasn't easy. I was frustrated by my inability to move as quickly as I wanted to but justified my disappointment by declaring that the pace was too slow here and that *it* needed to change. I wasn't able to see how it was *I* who needed to change if I wanted to be successful in this new country. When I eventually got past my ego's justifications by looking at the situation from a more vertical perspective, I began to understand how things were done rather than attempt to speed them up. I slowed down and achieved more than I had ever achieved in the past. After being in Canada for over ten years now, I am grateful that I was flexible enough to change and experience how, by putting my ego aside, I could achieve just as much if not more.

❖ Think of the last time that you justified your behavior only to find out at a later stage that you were procrastinating change. The next step is to be honest with yourself and recognize that what you are justifying now is based on fear and insecurity and the resistance to change. The final step is to decide whether you are going to continue fooling yourself or, pluck up the courage and do the right thing that will help you move forward.

7. Pride

Pride is also the workings of the ego and is the main hurdle that prevents many people from becoming more vertical. We are not talking about being "proud of" others here—for example, a parent being pleased or delighted by a son's or daughter's special achievements. What I refer to here is when people are arrogant or self-important, too proud to show that they have made a mistake, or boastful or superior when they have achieved something better than others.

The easiest way to know if your pride is ego driven is to check your motive. For example, ask yourself why you can't say that you're sorry, or why it's so important to you that people recognize your achievements. Make sure that you stay awake to potential justifications and other defense mechanisms that your ego will quickly call to its aid in convincing you of your righteousness. Only *you* can be brutally honest with yourself.

Where are you currently being influenced by your pride?

Dealing with the Ego

It is important that we understand and learn to deal with our ego because it is the biggest obstacle to becoming vertical and the biggest cause of conflict between human beings. Until we learn to deal with the ego, we will continue to experience inner and outer conflicts, superiority and inferiority, fear and insecurity, self-doubt, inflated pride, and inertia.

When we continue to feed into the needs of the ego, we allow it to grow and take control. This control by the ego explains why it is so difficult for people to change their habitual behaviors. It is like small children: if they are used to doing whatever they want, it is difficult to expect them to change and suddenly be disciplined. The longer you allow the ego to be in control, the harder it becomes to change that pattern. This change does not require a major struggle but, rather, the awareness and patience to redirect your attention toward more positive and constructive behaviors. By so doing, you begin to take control of your thoughts, choices, actions, and, ultimately, your life. When we learn how to deal with the ego effectively, we are able to act in a more vertical manner, to grow, and to express our full potential.

How the Ego Operates

To deal effectively with the ego, it helps if we can recognize how we *behave* when the ego is running the show and controlling our minds. There are five main behaviors that are apparent when we are acting out of ego: *fight, flight, freeze, deceive, and appease.* In situations where we are living horizontally and our ego feels threatened, one or all of these five ego behaviors will be activated.

- **Fight**—aggression, self-justification, anger, and opposition
- **Flight**—fleeing from uncomfortable or confronting situations, even when it's to our advantage to stand up for ourselves
- **Freeze**—getting stuck in a position and being unwilling to move from it
- **Deceive**—aligning with others for personal gain and selfish motives (This behavior may seem altruistic at first glance, but there is almost always an ulterior motive or a hidden agenda present.)
- **Appease**—trying to talk our way out or behave in a way that will please those who we believe have control over our fate

The Ego Uses Fear to Buy More Time

As we have already seen, fear is one of the ego's strongest weapons. Fear makes us feel separate and divided and resistant to change in the face of uncertainty. When it senses that its position may be threatened, the ego buys time by stimulating doubt and anxiety so that it can remain in control and not get swept away by hope and enthusiasm.

Figure 2

AUTHENTIC SELF or EGO

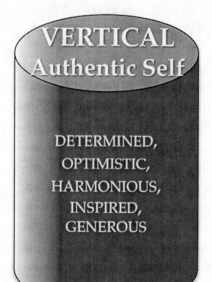

VERTICAL
Authentic Self

DETERMINED,
OPTIMISTIC,
HARMONIOUS,
INSPIRED,
GENEROUS

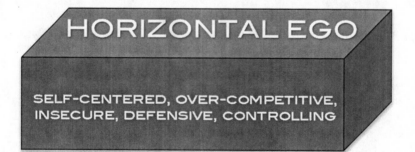

HORIZONTAL EGO

SELF-CENTERED, OVER-COMPETITIVE,
INSECURE, DEFENSIVE, CONTROLLING

You may have had a great insight, seen opportunity for change, or been excited about your future prospects only to be tripped up by the ego. Before you knew it, you were experiencing doubt, anxiety, and insecurity. The little voice of the ego (using your own voice) started to say things like, *What are you thinking about? You're too old for this!* Or, *You're too young for this!* Or, *You don't have enough money for this!* Or, *It's never been done before.* All this doubtful internal chatter happens incredibly fast, and in an instant, your dream, your vision, this potential for something great, has been squashed by the ego. You experience the excitement of the vertical potential on the one hand and the fear of the horizontal ego on the other. You may feel disappointed, or even inadequate, because the vertical part of you that wants to create and move forward has been overruled by the ego. If such incidents happen repeatedly, your self-esteem may become deflated, and on some deep level, you may feel impotent and despondent. The ego is so effective when it uses fear and sows doubt because we feel an immediate, unconscious, temporary relief for not having to take the chance, for not having to do something uncertain and risk losing something else. Because it is only temporary, however, we soon begin to experience all the negative feelings of inadequacy and the deepest hurt of all—the betrayal of the self.

❖ To better understand how the ego uses fear to buy more time, ask yourself the following questions:

1. *When did I last have a great dream or goal that deep down reflected what I really want to do?*
2. *If I did not act on that great dream or goal, how did I feel?*
3. *Do I tend to blame outside events or other people for my procrastination in making the change and moving forward?*

The Greatest Secret About the Ego

The ego part of us is not real. It is only our identification with it that makes it seem real for us. When we change our relationship to the ego by acknowledging that it's there, letting go of it, and refusing to identify with it, it loses its power over us. By stepping back and observing the ego as it goes through its various manipulations and acrobatics, we create space between it and our authentic self, which allows us to see the ego for the illusion it really is.

The Authentic, Vertical Self

At every moment, we make a choice between being horizontal (ego) or being more vertical (authentic). Choosing the ego suppresses life and causes conflict in our internal world and the world around us. The authentic self, on the other hand, is that creative part of us that wants to move forward, to learn, to grow, and to evolve. The authentic self is always vertical. This self lives in the vertical dimension, and when we choose it above the ego, we experience authentic motivation, authentic power, and an unlimited capacity for authentic action.

Choosing the most natural part of who you are, your authentic self, is a creative process that benefits and contributes to others around you. When we consistently choose to be vertical, we begin to experience a different form of existence that is extremely fulfilling because we know at a profound level that we are active participants in the process of life. We feel liberated and in touch with a higher purpose.

> *Freedom does not come automatically; it is achieved. And it is not gained in a single bound; it must be achieved each day.*
> —*Rollo May*

To determine whether your choice of action comes from the ego or the authentic self, check your motivation. When your motive comes from the authentic self, you no longer experience the separating, divisive, and self-preserving fears characteristic of your ego. Instead, you experience wholeness.

Being more vertical requires the courage to do the right thing even when you are tempted to do otherwise. It is being responsible for choosing power over force, truth over falsehood, humility over arrogance, and authenticity over ego. The more we nurture and reinforce the vertical habits, the more they strengthen and the easier it is to sustain them. The more we reinforce and support the horizontal and egotistic habits, the bigger they grow and the more difficult it becomes to free ourselves from the shackles of their attachments and ingrained dependencies.

Your motive will always tell you whether you are coming from ego or from authentic self.

The Canadian First Nations people have a wonderful legend that illustrates this perfectly. Here I use the title "Grandfather Tells," but it is also known as "The Wolves Within."

Grandfather Tells

An old grandfather said to his grandson, who came to him with anger at a friend who had done him an injustice, "Let me tell you a story.

"I, too, at times, have felt a great hate for those that have taken so much, with no sorrow for what they do.

"But hate wears you down and does not hurt your enemy. It is like taking poison and wishing your enemy would die. I have struggled with these feelings many times." He continued, "It is as if there are two wolves inside me. One is good and does no harm. He lives in harmony with all around him and does not take offense when no offense was intended. He will only fight when it is right to do so, and in the right way.

"But the other wolf, ah! He is full of anger. The littlest thing will set him into a fit of temper. He fights everyone, all the time, for no reason. He cannot think because his anger and hate are so great. It is helpless anger, for his anger will change nothing.

"Sometimes, it is hard to live with these two wolves inside me, for both of them try to dominate my spirit."

The boy looked intently into his grandfather's eyes and asked, "Which one wins, Grandfather?"

The grandfather smiled and quietly said, "The one I feed."

Our values are reflected in our behavior not in our words. Activating your true power requires recognizing your ego and its motivations and then choosing to live vertically.

Figure 3

The Ego vs. the Vertical Self

Ego (false self)	Vertical Self (authentic self)
Impure, selfish motive – seeks only for itself	Pure motive – always expressing the higher truth/purity
Thinks it already knows everything	Always open – ever inquiring
Small, limited context	Infinite context
Confusion	Clarity
Procrastinates	Passionate urgency
Constantly resists change	Thrives on change
Does not want to participate in selfless events or actions	Always ready to participate for the good of ALL
No commitment	Fully committed
False	Real
Manipulation	Collaboration
Inward	Outward
Desire	Service
How I feel	What is
I am unique/special	We are One/all
Protecting itself	Open and trusting
Control	Surrender
Denial	Acceptance
Fear	Courage
Untrustworthy – selfish motive	Absolutely trustworthy – selfless
Uses force because of weakness	Uses power because of strength
Hatred	Compassion
Ugliness	Beauty
My opinion	Truth

Chapter 4

Charge Your Quantum Magnet

When we are determined to live vertically and not be swayed by our ego's desires, we can tap into an unlimited reserve of universal energy to bolster our resolve. In this chapter, we explore how we can make this energy our own.

Over the past twenty years or so, there have been a number of significant scientific breakthroughs that have overturned many earlier concepts of the mind, matter, and form. At the turn of the twentieth century, quantum physics shook up many of the trusted theories that once defined our world and explained its workings (e.g., Newtonian

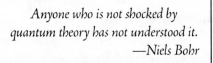

Anyone who is not shocked by quantum theory has not understood it.
—*Niels Bohr*

theory). Further developments in the field have given us a more interrelated and fluid vision of the physical world. Quantum mechanics has shown that things at the subatomic level operate in very mysterious ways.

This chapter aims at understanding what scientists and physicists are saying about these profound developments and, more importantly, how you can harness this knowledge to help activate your power to create and attract the life that you want.

The Body Is an Energy Field

Matter is not as solid as we perceive it to be; it is mostly empty space. If we explore matter at the subatomic level, we find a whole "world" of energy—particles and waves vibrating at different rates—dancing in space.

If we were to look at the body with an imaginary quantum microscope, we would first see the familiar cells of the body. Turning up the magnification of the microscope, we would see even smaller particles, such as atoms, and then, with still greater magnification, the nucleus of each atom with its protons and neutrons.

Going even deeper, at the subatomic level, we would see even smaller particles, jumping and wiggling between orbits around the nucleus, a kind of sea of vibrating energy. So we see, the human body at such a minute level is not a solid piece of matter, as we would normally understand it, but an energy field vibrating at a particular speed. As individuals, we are distinguished from each other by the pattern, density, and frequency at which our energy vibrates.

Karl Pribram, neurosurgeon and Professor at Stanford University, has proposed that there are links between quantum physics and the human mind. He suggests that the brain might function as a holograph, ordering energy patterns for us much as a holograph orders light. The body appears to us to be solid simply because the mind acts as a lens and converts the complex information it receives into a solid image.

Everything Is Energy

At the subatomic or quantum level then, everything is reduced to energy, like an unbroken, interconnected web, a kind of cosmic Internet. Our body is an energy field surrounded by other energy fields—from our immediate environments to our entire universe. More significantly, at the deepest, smallest level there is no distinction between the part and the whole: all is as one. This blurring of boundaries at the particle level points to the underlying connectivity between all things.

Taking Pribram's theory one step further, David Bohm, a quantum physicist and protégé of Albert Einstein, proposed that our entire universe may be a hologram, a huge field of electromagnetic frequencies with multiple levels of reality. Bohm used the analogy of a river to illustrate his theory:

The universe and all that is in it, are all part of an undivided whole. Look at the little eddies and whirlpools that often form in a river. At a glance such whirlpools appear to be separate things and possess individual qualities such as size, rate and direction of rotation. But careful scrutiny reveals that it is impossible to determine where any given whirlpool ends and the river begins. The universal tendency to fragment the world is responsible for many of our problems—in science, in our lives and in society.

Michael Talbot, author of *The Holographic Universe,* thought along the same lines, suggesting that, "All things in the universe are no more separate from one another than different patterns in an ornate carpet." From a quantum viewpoint, it is meaningless to think of any one thing as separate from any other thing.

Einstein himself had recognized earlier that two or more particles that have interacted in the past still exhibit strong correlations when measured later. This was later illustrated by the famous Aspect experiments conducted in the 1980s, which demonstrated that once-connected particles that were separated by vast distances remained somehow connected. If one particle was changed, the other also changed instantly.

In a similar fashion, an astounding experiment conducted with monkey colonies between 1952 and 1958 on the Japanese island of Koshima also pointed to quantum entanglement. When sweet potatoes were introduced to an isolated colony of macaque monkeys for the first time, the monkeys would not eat them because they were covered in sand and dirt. Eventually, one young monkey discovered that if she washed the potato in water, the problem was solved, and the potato could be eaten. Once this was "learned," other young monkeys in this colony followed suit and washed the potatoes before eating them. By 1958, the adults were imitating the young ones. Surprisingly, according to anecdote, once a certain critical number of monkeys learned the washing technique, the practice was adopted by the entire colony within a very short time.

This was impressive in itself, but what followed was astonishing. It appeared that suddenly, the knowledge of washing potatoes to make them acceptable as a food source seemed to be learned remotely by other monkey colonies on the mainland and on different islands— that is, with no physical contact between the monkey colonies.

In another example of connection over time/distance, in the 1920s, Professor McDougall of Harvard University tested twenty generations of rats on the same water maze. To his amazement, the twentieth generation was able to complete the maze ten times more quickly than the first generation. Neither he nor his contemporaries believed that knowledge could be transmitted genetically, so Scottish scientist F. Crew duplicated the experiment. Imagine his astonishment when he discovered that his *first* generation of rats finished the maze as quickly as the last generation tested by Professor McDougall, with some even completing the maze immediately, as if they already knew it. How had this "learning" crossed the Atlantic to an entirely new population of rats?

Theory now suggests that when a certain threshold is reached—a "critical mass"—the particular knowledge or skill learned is seemingly miraculously available to all others in the population, regardless of how much physical distance separates them. Psychologist Carl Jung might have explained this via his concept of the collective unconscious, as would the current Princeton University–based *Global Consciousness Project*. Shamans and spiritual teachers across the ages have long recognized the interconnectedness of all things, often seeing mankind at the center of the web and thus able to affect every other part of the universe.

This interconnectedness has significant implications for the way we must see the world. We are indeed mind, body, and spirit together. It thus follows that harming someone else is actually harming ourselves. In the same way, judging or blaming others makes no sense, since we are all connected. Deepak Chopra, the bestselling author of *Ageless Body Timeless Mind*, *Creating Affluence*, *Quantum Healing* and many other well-known books, expresses the same notion of interconnectedness with his words, *"The environment is your extended body."*

It seems that quantum physics may begin to provide a scientific explanation for how knowledge, information, or intelligence can move through the quantum energy field that connects us all.

The Mind Is not in the Brain

Since our entire being is composed of energy, it follows that information can be exchanged between the brain and the rest of the body. What we call the mind, therefore, is not necessarily somewhere inside our brain: it is in the energy field of the body and permeates both the brain and physical body. Consciousness may be shared by all cells of the body.

In fact, the human energy field can respond before the brain does. A researcher and professor of kinesiology at UCLA, Valerie Hunt, studied this phenomenon by taking simultaneous electromyograph (EMG) readings of the human body's energy field and electroencephalogram (EEG) readings of the brain. She discovered that when the researcher makes a loud noise or flashes a bright light, the EMG registers this stimulus before it is noted on the EEG. This led Hunt to conclude that the brain is, "just a real good computer."

On a very simple level, we have all experienced times when our emotions and bodies act in harmony. Guilt may leave you feeling sick to your stomach. You may have been unable to eat from worry while waiting for crucial test results. Or, perhaps you can remember a time when you were wildly infatuated with someone, and your heart beat faster each time that person walked into the room. These are all illustrations of the connection between your "mind" and body cells.

Scientists have also discovered that there is intelligence in every single cell of the body. This startling discovery has supported branches of science, like human stem-cell research, where undifferentiated stem cells, or now even induced pluripotent state cells (iPSCs), can be prompted to become whatever cell type is needed (lung or liver cells, for example) to replace damaged or sick cells in a patient.

Thoughts Are Real Forces

Brain activity can be viewed with technology such as Positron Emission Tomography (PET), Magnetic Resonance Imaging (MRI), and EEG testing—all procedures that measure biological activity through the skull and reveal the human brain at work. These brain scans are used by scientists and doctors to detect energy patterns for diagnostic purposes, such as damage after a stroke or the presence of ADHD (attention deficit hyperactivity disorder). By extension, we can see that our thoughts, simple brain activity, can be traced as a pattern of vibration in the energy field.

All experiences—real or simply conceptual, dreams, ideas, or physical sensations—are ultimately reduced to the same common energy patterns in the brain that we can see with scientific instruments. How does the mind distinguish between real and imagined events then? At this pure energy level, ideas and events are equally real, and, therefore, it is possible that thoughts will manifest as realities in the physical body and in the physical world.

Next, we will see how your thoughts can make a difference to your life.

When we change our thinking, we change our reality.

The Quantum Magnet (The Law of Attraction)

You may already be familiar with the Law of Attraction, either through books or articles or the Internet, or perhaps you have seen the well-known film or book *The Secret,* which came out a few years ago.

According to the Law of Attraction, entities that have a similar energetic vibrational frequency attract each other. So, not only are we made of energy, with thoughts of energy, we also attract other energy to ourselves. Think of yourself as a kind of magnet that attracts "like energy" to itself. We'll call it the "quantum magnet," because it works very powerfully at a deep level. For most people, this same-energy attraction occurs unconsciously, but it has the potential to become very powerful when it is used as a deliberate and conscious act.

What you attract into your life is determined by what you send out—the messages, the vibrations, and the energy. Understanding this principle is fundamental to activating your power. The more focused your energy, and the clearer the messages that you send, the clearer the energy that you attract will be and the more likely you are to attract the experiences you want in your life.

If, however, you are not very clear or focused, have many distracting thoughts and conflicting and incongruent beliefs, the energy that will be attracted to you will also be jumbled and dissipated. In other words, your own lack of clarity, purpose, or focus is the main source of most of your inner conflicts and lack of fulfillment. Without clarity, there is confusion, and when we are confused, we tend to experience anxiety or feel overwhelmed, which makes us feel even more powerless.

Furthermore, if your thoughts are chaotic and filled with negativity and fear, you will manifest chaos, negativity, and fear in your outer world and in your life in general. On the other hand, an inner world that is filled with joy, peace, and love corresponds directly to a life rich in joy, peace, and love.

We are not *discovering* our world, but rather, we are continually participating in its creation.

Whatever you believe, you are right (according to you).

Our thoughts, our intentions, and our will are real forces, and because they are potentially very powerful forces, they need to be used with care. Not only do they impact on our universe, they shape us in the sense that they actively alter our energy field.

Many spiritual healers have reported that they are able to see illnesses in the energy field (or aura) of other

> *Your own mind is a sacred enclosure into which nothing harmful can enter except by your permission.*
> —*Ralph Waldo Emerson*

people. These have not yet manifested in the physical world but will do so unless the core pattern in the blueprint of the energy field is altered.

❖ Think for a moment about the possible effect of a continuous flood of negative thoughts into your energy field. Do you know some people with whom you can spend only five minutes before you feel like your energy has been sucked out of you? With what type of energy do you think they are vibrating? Would you say they are more vertical or more horizontal when that happens?

When I ask these questions in my corporate seminars, there is always a chuckle from the participants, and I often see people look at each other in agreement about a person in their company who resembles that description. Conversely, I am sure that you also know people who are usually enthusiastic, optimistic, and vibrating with positive energy. These individuals often attract positive events into their lives and are regarded as "lucky." Imagine the different experiences of life that these two kinds of people have. Think of the health implications of each scenario.

The most important point we can extrapolate from these examples is that we can choose how we use our quantum magnets, and it is a choice that we can make every day, every hour, and every minute. We can choose the positive or the negative, the focused or the scattered, the vertical or the horizontal; the outcomes of each choice are very clear.

How to Attract the Life You Want

Many people fall into a misconception about the Law of Attraction and believe that merely by thinking about something they want, the drums will roll and they will attract these things into their lives, like fruit flies to fruit. I don't believe that there is any type of magic wand that can make that happen. Rather, *we*—the ones who have the power to choose what to focus on, what to pay attention to, and what to direct our energies toward—are the ones who actually make it happen.

I am a strong believer in the Law of Attraction and have used it very successfully in both my personal and professional lives, but I believe that the reason it has worked for me is because *I* made it work rather than *it* just happened. What I have observed in my own experience, and in the study of many highly successful people, is that our level of attraction and what we manifest in our lives is largely influenced by three key factors.

Factor 1: Where You Are on the Horizontal or Vertical Levels

The more vertical you are, the more filled with hope and optimism, the greater the likelihood that you will resonate with frequencies that are similar to yours and, therefore, attract situations, events, and people that have a similar energy to yours. At the vertical level, you will spend more time with positive people, grow more, achieve goals at faster rates than others on lower levels, and be happier and more positive about life in general. Just like the saying, "Birds of a feather flock together," like attracts like at an energetic level.

People who are vibrating at lower horizontal levels, however, are likely to feel dissatisfied with their lot in life, whether that means their relationship at home, their lack of fulfillment at work, or their financial situation. Some people seem to experience one negative event after another, knocking through their lives like a game of dominos. Outsiders might attribute this to bad luck, but understanding the force of the quantum magnet, we can see that there are forces at play that go beyond luck and that it is *we* who direct that luck or lack of it in our lives.

Despite all the good intentions that a person at the horizontal level may have about attracting better circumstances, for as long as he is stuck at that level, his vibrational frequency will continue to attract more of what he currently has (or doesn't have), and the cycle will continue. The only way out is to move up the levels, to move to a more vertical plane.

Factor 2: What You Are Paying Most Attention To (Focus)

The second factor affecting what your energy attracts relates to your *attention,* or where you place most of your focus. The American National Science Foundation has found that, on average, we have between 15,000 to 60,000 thoughts per day. Imagine the internal processing that's going on in your head, and add to that, the external noise and demands for your attention you are subjected to at work, at home, and through the different media channels. You can see how easy it is to be distracted and how challenging it is to stay focused on one task at a time with all that competition for your attention.

People who are able to stay focused for longer periods of time are generally able to achieve better results in a fraction of the time that it takes others who are not as focused. The more vertical we are, the less distracted we are, since most of our attention is in the present moment.

People who spend the majority of their time at the horizontal levels, however, are more prone to distractions, since their minds are constantly reacting to external stimuli such as events, other people, or their own thoughts and feelings. Furthermore, since they spend a lot of their time thinking about past events and the future, their attention is easily moved from the task at hand. The pursuit of a goal is often arduous and painful due to the start/stop movements along the desired path. Looking too often in the rearview mirror seriously hampers your navigational capabilities!

The more you are able to *focus* on the goal or what it is that you desire, the quicker you will manifest it.

Factor 3: The Action You Take

The process of creation is thought—word—deed. Without the last step, deed (action), very little will be achieved. The more you think about it, the more you talk about it, the more you focus on it, and the clearer you are about what "it" is, the greater your potential for acting to create that magic we call the Law of Attraction. Notice the

> For to whomsoever much is given, of him shall be much required.
> —Luke 12:48

level of involvement required. It isn't mere intention, a wave of a magic wand, that brings you all your wishes. It is *you* who make it happen by vibrating at the vertical level, using absolute focus, and then taking action toward it.

❖ Consider a major achievement that you have accomplished, and trace the process from its inception. Did it magically happen, or did you first think about it? Were you blasé about it, or did you pay a lot of attention to it, talk about it, and think even more about it, plan for it, and then do something about it?

You can see how your active participation in the entire process gives you the capacity to make things happen in your life that go way beyond what you even imagined possible. It *is* possible, but *you* have to start the process.

**The energy we send out determines what
we attract into our lives.**

Mastering Your Own Mind

Successful people, whether they are top athletes or entrepreneurs, have mastered the power of both their conscious and subconscious minds to produce their success. Many of us haven't tapped into the unlimited potential of our minds because we haven't been taught how our minds actually work.

Our minds are made up of two distinct processes: the conscious and the subconscious minds. When we vigorously

> *Within the seed of your desire is everything necessary for it to blossom to fulfillment. And Law of Attraction is the engine that does the work. Your work is just to give it a fertile growing place in order to expand.*
> *—Jerry and Esther Hicks*

focus our efforts on creating unity between the conscious and subconscious minds, we can achieve a greater sense of happiness and success in our lives.

Dr. Joseph Murphy, author of *The Power of Your Subconscious Mind,* has a wonderful analogy to explain the relationship between the conscious and subconscious minds. He likens our physical body to a ship with a captain (the conscious mind) and a crew (the subconscious). Just as a boat can't go anywhere without a captain, your body won't go anywhere without someone to give it directions.

Your Conscious Mind: The Captain of the Ship

Your conscious mind is like the ship's captain, who uses his instruments and his experience to make decisions and then issues orders to his crew. Like the captain, the conscious mind has the ability to think, decide, and act. It receives information, evaluates it through rational process, accepts or rejects it, and then filters that information to the subconscious mind.

Your Subconscious Mind: The Crew of the Ship

If your conscious mind is the captain of the ship, your subconscious mind is the crew. Like the crew of a ship, your subconscious mind takes orders without question or evaluation. It does not differentiate good from bad, right from wrong, or even real from imagined; it merely obeys. A well-trained crew does not need to be told how to carry out the orders; the captain simply trusts that they will be done. In much the same way, your conscious mind hands over decisions, thoughts, and ideas to the subconscious for execution.

Your Thoughts: The Captain's Orders

Whenever orders are fed to the subconscious mind, it acts on them and carries them out, even if they can lead you into danger. Because the crew does not evaluate the orders it receives, the quality and safety of the ship can only be as good as the quality of orders being communicated from the captain. In the same way, your own thoughts affect you indiscriminately. When you think, *I'm successful and content*, that is an order issued to your crew. Conversely, when you tell yourself, *I'm unfortunate and inadequate,* your subconscious mind will make that happen, too. The quality of orders, or "autosuggestions," you give your subconscious mind will determine the level of success you are able to produce for yourself.

The Buddha said it with great clarity over 2,500 years ago: "We are what we think. All that we are arises with our thoughts. With our thoughts, we make the world."

In other words, by changing your thinking, you can change your reality, and by changing your reality, you can change your life!

Part II

Activate Your Power

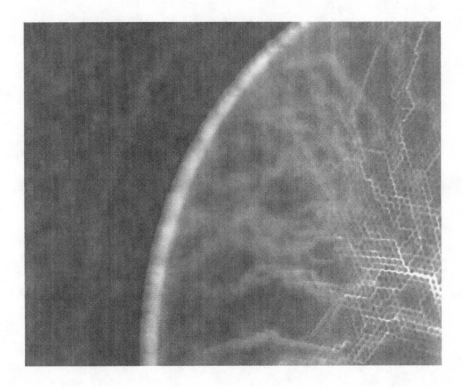

Chapter 5

Manage Your Emotions

Even if we place a substantial amount of effort on directing our thoughts and actions toward charging our quantum magnets, our efforts will be to no avail if we ignore the "rogue" element of our own emotions and the role they play.

What Emotions Are at Work in Your Life?

To begin, let's do a short exercise to find out which energies and emotions are being attracted to your quantum magnet.

❖ Below you will find a list of emotions and states of mind in simple alphabetical order (see figure 4). As you read through them, underline those emotions or states that are most prevalent in your life. Do this three times, perhaps using a different color each time, to highlight the dominant emotions that relate to three important areas of your life:

1. Me at home
2. Me at work
3. My entire business
   (if you are in a small business), or
   My team, department, or division
   (if you work in a big company).

Think about how you feel at work, for example. Do you feel _uncertainty_ or _optimism_? Perhaps there is fierce competition to get ahead at your place of work, or perhaps there are rumors that the company will be downsizing or other changes are about to take place. Or perhaps you have just returned from an inspiring company weekend retreat, and you can relate more to the words _hopefulness_ and _excitement_.

Figure 4

Emotions and States of Mind

Abundance	Euphoria	Loneliness
Acceptance	Excitement	Love
Aggression	Exhaustion	Misery
Anger	Fatigue	Neutrality
Anxiety	Fear	Optimism
Apathy	Focus	Overwhelmed
Blame	Forgiveness	Pain
Bliss	Freedom	Peace
Boredom	Grief	Positivity
Confidence	Guilt	Powerlessness
Contentment	Happiness	Pride
Courage	Harmony	Regret
Craving	Hate	Resentment
Demanding	Hopefulness	Sadness
Depression	Hopelessness	Satisfaction
Desire	Hostile	Shame
Despair	Humiliation	Stress
Disappointment	Incompetent	Trust
Disrespect	Inspiration	Uncertainty
Ease	Joy	Willingness

Once you have completed your selection, write down the one emotion for each of the three categories that *most* represents where you are right now. (You can repeat the same emotion more than once, if necessary.)

Category	Dominant Emotion
Me at work	_____
Me at home	_____
My business/team	_____

Look at the answers you have written down. What insights can you gain from seeing the single emotion that most represents your current state in these important areas of your life? Perhaps the emotions that affect one category are also spilling over into other aspects of your life. You now know that it is your responsibility to manage the energy you put out. But can you manage your emotions? And if so, how?

Choose the Vertical Response

Most of the time, people react automatically to events and circumstances, according to established patterns of response that they have learned over many years. Once these patterns of response have become habits, they are difficult to change.

One of the key starting points in becoming more vertical is the understanding that in *every* instance, you have a choice of how you can respond, both emotionally and physically. You can either choose to come from your ego or "small-self" (your horizontal self), or you can choose to step back and take a more vertical perspective. This choice underlies everything. Whether you realize it, you are constantly making choices between a small-picture perspective and a big-picture perspective in every situation.

Seeing life from the small-picture perspective means looking at the situation from a limited, personalized perspective only. If I relate everything I see to my immediate feelings, everything becomes very personal, and I am likely to react to protect myself. Consider the following example:

For the past few years, Pauline had received good ratings in her performance reviews and was regarded as a positive contributor to her team and organization. During her latest performance review meeting, however, where five key performance indicators were evaluated, her direct manager gave her an average review and told her that she has more potential than she displayed over the past year. Pauline was also told specifically that she needs to improve her performance in two of the areas under review. Pauline had not expected her review to go this way and was surprised that she only received an "average" performer rating rather than "good" or even "high" as she had in previous years.

From the horizontal perspective, Pauline would be very upset and may even feel that she was picked on. She would feel too embarrassed to share her review with her work colleagues (as they would normally do) and would be in a reactive mode. Her reactive mode would likely lead her to feel angry and resentful toward her manager. She might start to say negative and harmful things about him to her colleagues to make herself feel better and ease her feelings of hurt and inadequacy. If Pauline continued on this negative spiral, she would ultimately end up disengaged and performing poorly.

From a vertical perspective, Pauline would have a very different experience. She might still feel surprised and even upset immediately after the review, but taking the big picture perspective, she would take responsibility for her performance and choose to do something positive and constructive about it.

Pauline would start to seek for ways she could improve. Her first step would be to draw up an action plan for the next twelve months, in which she would commit to accelerating her development—not only in the two key areas that she did poorly on but also in the other three areas that are evaluated every year.

In addition, she would arrange for a meeting with her manager to share her plans with him. She would also request that he meet with her at least every two weeks to provide her with specific coaching toward helping her excel in her professional capacity. Pauline would ensure that she received regular feedback on her performance and would make the necessary improvements throughout the year. Her levels of engagement and motivation would *increase* due to her focus and determination to succeed.

By choosing a vertical response to the same original scenario, Pauline would avoid the negative effects of becoming angry and resentful. Instead, by moving away from those detrimental emotions, she would be able to see how a "bad" performance review could ultimately improve her work situation.

No matter how you have chosen to respond until now, you are always free to make the best choice in this moment and from now on. This is tremendously exciting! You are not bound by your previous choices. Although you may still feel the negative effects of those choices, you are now free and able to rise above choosing a negative reaction.

Reacting vs. Responding

So far we have used the words "react" and "respond" as if they were interchangeable. But understanding the difference between these two words will further help you to manage your emotions.

To react means exactly that—to *re-act* (to act again as you have done in the past). Reaction is an automatic answer to a stimulus or situation. There is no contemplation or consideration, just a knee-jerk reaction that often leads to remorse and regret. In the example above, taking the small-picture, personalized perspective is reacting.

When you "respond," on the other hand, you offer a considered answer to the stimulus or situation and then behave accordingly. Responding means that you have created sufficient space to consider what the optimal response should be. The big-picture concern in the example above is a response.

Remember: You can choose whether you "react" or "respond" in each and every situation.

In order to understand what causes some people to react to stimuli while others, exposed to the same triggers, respond more carefully, we can look first at how our physical brain affects our behavior.

The Brain and How We React/Respond

When a stimulus occurs, usually in the form of an external trigger, a signal enters the center of the brain at the *thalamus*, which acts like an air traffic controller. The thalamus sends information to various parts of the brain, particularly "up" to the *prefrontal cortex* (PFC) and "down" to the *amygdala*.

The PFC, or CEO of the brain, controls higher-level thinking processes, such as logic, analysis, and decision making. The amygdala, sometimes described as the emotional center or the guard dog of the mind, plays a major role in emotional responses. This almond-shaped neuro-structure is involved in producing and responding to nonverbal signs of anger, avoidance, defensiveness, and fear. It reacts incredibly fast to incoming stimuli and is sometimes also referred to as the fight or flight part of the brain.

Successful interactions require a certain amount of conscious intention using both the PFC and the amygdala to create a blended response. When the right blend of thinking and control from the PFC is combined with the right amount of emotion from the amygdala, a person should respond successfully to a particular event (stimulus) by executing an appropriate action pattern. Fortunately, in most cases, the PFC is able to exert control over the amygdala's reactions and help the person avoid what Daniel Goleman (author of *Emotional Intelligence: Why It Can Matter More Than IQ*) calls "amygdala hijacking." However, when something, such as stress, interferes with the functioning of the PFC, the probability of making an inappropriate decision increases.

The initial release of neurotransmitters and hormones into a person's system after an event affects the major brain systems. Too much stress "turns off" the PFC, resulting in a drop in its ability to control the amygdala. Stress even temporarily reduces IQ! At the same time, the increased stress "turns on" the amygdala, creating an overly sensitive, heightened state of emotion. When this happens, we lose a significant amount of our ability to control our emotions and become not only temporarily cognitively impaired but also less emotionally intelligent. (A person who consistently demonstrates the ability to be self-aware, to self-manage, and display social awareness and skills at appropriate times and situations is regarded as emotionally intelligent.)

Don't let stress hijack your brain!

Knowing this makes it easier to understand why highly (mentally) intelligent people sometimes behave in ways that are dysfunctional and emotionally juvenile. It also points to the need for continued emotional development and the expansion of our emotional capacity to deal with stressful and diverse situations.

Changing Old Negative Programs

Not only does our capacity to respond depend on the interplay between our emotional and thinking parts of the brain, but our previous experiences also play a large part in how we process the constant stimuli—events, situations, and information—we receive. Often before we even consciously think about it, the stimuli enter the brain and move along an existing recognized pathway, generating a programmed response.

Figure 5 shows how information entering our brains is greeted with two questions without our conscious awareness: *What does this mean?* and *How should I respond?* Almost instantaneously, we answer these questions and respond/react accordingly, sliding the stimuli down a well-worn path of automatic response/reaction.

How are these pathways created?

Suppose that when you were young, a frustrated teacher told you that you were not going to amount to much when you grew up if you didn't concentrate better. A few years later, an impatient uncle tried to teach you to ride a bicycle, but you wobbled and fell; he shrugged his shoulders and said you were useless. Then, when you were twelve, you had a bullying neighbor, who used to mock and taunt you, saying that you had no friends. When you were seventeen, you had a girlfriend or boyfriend you adored, but that person left you for someone else, and you felt even more inadequate. And on it went …

Repeated experiences can become imprinted in our minds as a negative response pathway. Certain events create a program of neuro-associations in our minds, and other subsequent events reinforce and validate the original program that was imprinted (such as a belief in one's inadequacy, for example).

Now, imagine that it's many years later. You have probably long since forgotten (at least on a conscious level) most of the little incidents that created your individual programs of neuro-associations. But they are imprinted in your mind, nonetheless; the path has been worn and is waiting until the right stimulus comes along to trigger a negative response. One day, someone says something disrespectful, and the pathway is opened. Your stored negative program is reactivated, and those old painful memories move closer to the surface. Before you know it, you instinctively react with anger, frustration, or even fear.

Does this sound familiar? Have you ever felt while in an argument that the other person knew exactly what buttons to push to make you angry? She seemed to know exactly what would trigger an angry reaction. Or he had instinctively learned to recognize your painful or sensitive imprinted pathways.

The Importance of Perspective

In the previous example, the stimulus itself (a disrespectful comment) was relatively harmless. And yet, an old response path was instantly opened in answer to both

> *Never fear shadows, it simply means that there is light shining somewhere nearby.*
> —Ruth E. Renkel

reception questions: *What does this mean?* and *How should I respond?* The answer to the first question (*I am inadequate*) provided the answer to the second (*with anger, frustration, anxiety, or pain*). Both responses were embedded deeply in the past, in the emotional memory. This caused an exaggeratedly negative reaction toward the other person. You might even have blamed the other person for your resulting negative reaction and emotions: *You made me do this. You made me feel terrible, rejected, unappreciated, angry.*

When we understand the underlying neuro-associations, however, we know that casting blame is pointless. The way we process the information that we receive determines how we respond to it. The outside stimulus is simply a trigger, and we can choose what it means to us and how to respond to it.

Overlaying this experience on the vertical/horizontal model, we find that it is our perspective that determines our experience. If your mode is primarily horizontal, you are more likely to react automatically in ways that you may regret. If you are coming from a more vertical perspective, many potential triggers or negative situations will have very little adverse impact.

The quality of your experience is determined by your *perception* of the experience. Change the perspective, and you change the experience. This means that when you change your perception or perspective to the vertical, your entire experience of life becomes different—less painful, more fulfilling. No matter what the events or stimuli, you can exercise your power to determine what an event means to you and how you choose to respond to it. We examine this in greater detail in the following chapter.

Figure 5

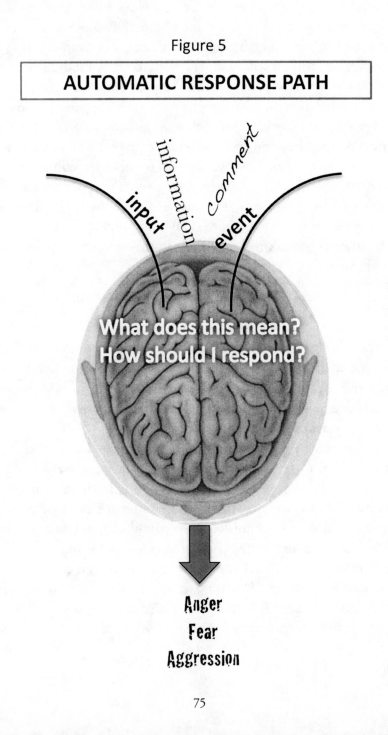

AUTOMATIC RESPONSE PATH

input information comment event

What does this mean?
How should I respond?

Anger
Fear
Aggression

Responding Positively

Let's look at an example of an alternate response to the same type of trigger. Suppose you were the person who had received so many negative messages throughout your childhood. Again, years later you receive a disrespectful comment: your manager at work accuses you of preparing a bad presentation. He delivered it and it didn't go very well, even though, in your opinion, the presentation itself was fine.

This time though, you recognize what is happening and you manage to ask yourself, *What is actually happening here?* From your vertical perspective, you see that your manager's comment means that he is frustrated and angry at himself for not succeeding with the presentation. He is using you as a scapegoat, taking out the negative feedback he received from *his* manager on you. Without attacking back in your own defense, you choose to respond by acknowledging his frustration and asking how he thinks the next presentation could be improved.

Your perception, and your perspective, determine your experience.

The more you exercise your power to choose not to "react," the more you will begin to develop new programs and responses that are productive. By creating new neuro-associations, you are taking a very important step toward activating your power. It is possibly the single most important step you can take.

The most amazing discovery about neuro-associations is that we can transform them and even create new ones for ourselves. If you get involved in an incident that would normally trigger a negative response, you do not have to follow the automatic negative reactive path; you can simply acknowledge the stimulus. And you can follow the two unconscious greetings—*What does this mean?* and *How should I respond?*—with further, constructive questions. You can break the old pathway by asking, "*How can I learn from this? Can I do anything with this information? Is it useful? Do I need to change something?*"

You may be surprised by the answers you discover:

Maybe I can learn something from this.

Maybe the other person has had a bad day, and I will not let that influence me.

Perhaps this incident is a lesson for me to be more tolerant and patient.

With this process, you will develop immunity to becoming automatically upset, angry, or frustrated. Instead of allowing an outside trigger to have a negative impact, you create a new program, a new response path. Now you will find that your interior dialogue sounds more constructive and positive than it would have before. For example:

I am okay. Right now, people at work around me are fearing for their jobs due to the downturn in the economy, and, therefore, they are behaving in irrational and disrespectful ways. I am not buying into it and refuse to participate in this hysteria. My focus is on what is working in my job right now and what I can do to make it work even better. I'm intelligent and sensible, and can respond in an effective and professional way.

"Thank You for Sharing!"

I have found that a useful technique for avoiding negative automatic reactions is to acknowledge the stimulus by addressing it directly. When I am aware of the ego reacting in me, I either acknowledge it by silently smiling, or in my head I say, *Thank you for sharing!* Next, I examine the stimulus objectively, asking myself what I will choose to do with this information. The best answer that I usually come up with is to keep the positive and disregard the negative. In this way, I move forward, strengthened with additional information, instead of becoming bogged down in a cycle of energy-draining emotion and lower-level response.

The smile or phrase is a powerful mechanism for staying in control of any situation that fits neatly into our old pathways. It allows us to bypass the primeval arousal center in our brain, remain in control of our emotional reaction, and dispassionately decide on appropriate new response paths.

In brief, the process is:

1. Acknowledge the stimulus without judgment: Smile or say, "Thank you for sharing," or, "I acknowledge you," or whatever else works for you.
2. Ask: *"What do I choose to do with this information?"*
3. Choose to create a new positive program. And move on.

This process of reprogramming response paths is illustrated in figure 6.

The result? Ultimately, you will experience far more pleasant and positive emotions: empowerment, confidence, and contentment. Remember, the power is in your hands.

Face Your Fears

Finally, to be truly free from the directive force of our emotions, we need to address one of the most powerful feelings of all: fear. We must learn to face all our fears, and confront with confidence anything that comes our way. We also need to face everything about ourselves and about all our relationships.

> *The conquering of fear is the beginning of wisdom.*
> —J. M. Cousteau

Facing and overcoming fear can bring great personal strength and a sense of victory. If you are not prepared to face your demons, you will forever hide from your reality and avoid or deny the truth. Growth, change, and progress toward your higher purpose will remain too intimidating and unattainable.

Fear of failure is a huge obstacle for most of us. We want to do things, but we are too afraid of the consequences. And whenever we are afraid to do something, we allocate more power to fear than to ourselves; we give away our strength. Fear wins the battle. If you are afraid of negative consequences, you will never be able to see the big picture. Instead, you will be forever defensive and spend most of your energy maintaining a cocoon of "security."

Maintenance of this cocoon usually leads to a great deal of frustration, insecurity, and very often, anger. We get stuck in ambivalence: on the one hand, we want to do something, but on the other, we're afraid of what might happen if we took action—or if we did not.

Figure 6

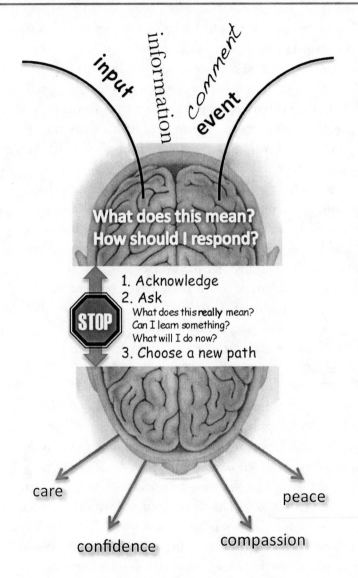

RE-PROGRAMMING RESPONSE PATHS

input
information
comment
event

What does this mean?
How should I respond?

STOP

1. Acknowledge
2. Ask
   What does this **really** mean?
   Can I learn something?
   What will I do now?
3. Choose a new path

care

peace

confidence

compassion

Do you remember the example I gave in chapter 3 about my disastrous eighth-grade presentation? That experience haunted me until I finally decided to face my fear by working on my confidence and presentation skills. I knew that in order to be successful, I would need to become an effective communicator. I got to work, enrolled in a presentation skills workshop that they were offering at Unilever, and asked my manager if I could deliver as many of her presentations as possible. What was once a fear began to turn into a challenge that I was meeting head-on. Some of my early presentations were unsuccessful, but as I continued to face my fear, I improved and started to feel more and more confident in front of the audience. After many presentations, I began to really enjoy myself up there and was having fun doing it. A few years later, during a presentation to a group of 1,200 people at Sun City in South Africa, I felt I was finally in my element. I had experienced the elation that comes from conquering a fear.

In hindsight, it wasn't only my presentation skills that improved; I also enhanced my interpersonal skills and my ability to connect with others. I came to realize how my fears were self-created and were not based on anything other than my own beliefs and past conditioning. Facing my fear paid off!

We can't have inner peace if we have constant conflict waging inside us. *I want to do it, but I'm afraid I'll fail, so I won't. No, I do want to do it! But what if things don't work out?* Some people spend their whole lives fighting this battle and never winning.

Put Down Your Rock

Even if you have determined that from this day forth you will face everything and respond without reacting, you may find it difficult to be truly vertical if you are bent over with a heavy load of unresolved emotional issues, which most people refer to as *baggage.*

Your ability to activate your power can be severely hampered by the emotional weight you have accumulated over time. I refer to this load as "the rock" that we carry on our backs. This rock represents the thoughts you have been hiding, the emotions you have been suppressing, or the feelings or events you have been keeping secret. These are energy draining, but as soon as you have identified them and are willing to face them, you can start to eliminate the energy wasters from your life.

Don't waste energy carrying around emotional weight
—put down the rock!

There is a Zen story about two monks crossing a river. They meet a beautiful young girl, who asks them for help crossing the river. The older monk picks her up and crosses the river, while the younger monk looks on in shock (as monks are supposed to avoid contact with women). A mile or so down the river, the younger monk is still in shock and can't stop thinking about the older monk's behavior. He turns to the old monk and says in a flabbergasted tone, "How could you pick up that girl when you know that we are forbidden contact with women?" The older monk turned to the young monk and said, "I crossed the river with that girl a mile ago and left her there, yet you still carry her."

What are you still carrying?

Unburden Yourself in Five Steps

There is a simple and quick exercise that I do to offload the rock from my back and feel free from my own accumulated baggage. This exercise consists of five steps:

❖ *Putting Down the Rock*

Step 1: Find a pen and paper and a quiet and comfortable place to sit where you will not be disturbed by your phone or by any other distraction.

Step 2: Focus on your desired emotional state for three to five minutes (e.g., focused, peaceful, engaged, etc.), and pay special attention to the thoughts and feelings that arise.

Step 3: Identify where your troubling thoughts and feelings are coming from (e.g., specific situation at work, specific situation at home), and observe them from a third-person perspective (*he* or *she* is feeling ...), detached and from the outside.

Step 4: Now, move into a second-person position and ask your own thoughts and feelings what they are trying to communicate to you (What are *you* to tell me?). Listen attentively, and write down the message and insights that you have gleaned from this question.

Step 5:   Finally, from the first-person perspective, ask yourself what alternative thoughts and feelings you should focus on to move forward (What do *I* need to focus on now?) and then get into that experience as though it were happening now.

In addition, I highly recommend that you create a daily ritual for understanding your emotions, and practice it for as long as you need it. This ritual should serve to remind you of your commitment to activating your power through managing your emotions. As an example of a daily ritual, you could record every situation that has occurred during the day that caused you to feel unease or discomfort. Then, before the day is over, make the time to go through your list and do the Putting Down the Rock exercise.

Chapter 6

Change Your Outlook

Why is it that some people achieve so much in a short lifetime while others don't? Look at Thomas Edison with all his inventions (over 1,000 patented), Leonardo da Vinci, Bill Gates, Steve Jobs, Richard Branson; the list could go on and on. What is the factor that makes the difference? Is it all about intellect? Is it about luck? Intellect, skill, and even being born at the right time in the right place certainly help, but they are not enough to make all the difference.

As we saw in chapter 4, everything in the physical universe is made up of energy. We, too, are bundles of energy, creating through wishes and desires and in constant energy exchange with one another. It therefore stands to reason that if we truly want to activate our power, we need to manage our energy effectively.

Even when we know what is the right thing to do, many of us still don't manage to do it. We commonly justify ourselves with our busy lives. Have you ever heard people complain that they don't have enough time because there are so many things they have to do each day?

Often it's our partner or children who bear the brunt of it. Our children might ask, *"Can you come and play with me? Please?"* Often, the answer is, *"Not now, honey. I'm really busy; there are things that I have to do first."*

Worse, the answer might sometimes be phrased in the form of sarcasm (usually the result of needs not being met over a long period): *"Oh, I suppose I will have to take you kids to the park. As usual, your father is too busy doing something else!"*

The Energy Factor

I believe that besides talent, intellect, charm, and luck, *energy* is the underlying factor that makes the difference between mastery and mediocrity.

Imagine that each morning when you wake up, you have around 100 kilowatts of pure energy available for you to enjoy and to create with. By the time you get to work, about 10 percent of that energy has already been consumed by preparing for work, the traffic or the commute to work, and the settling down to start work. If you are like most people, with unresolved issues or a rock that you carry around with you, you will consume another 10 to 15 percent of your energy to carry that rock. (You may sometimes even feel the weight of that rock translated into physical stress in your back and shoulders!)

By ten o'clock in the morning, about 30 percent of your energy has already been used up, and you have only 70 percent left to carry you through the rest of the day. During the workday, you have to deal with everyday matters that consume even more energy. By lunchtime, about 60 percent of your kilowatts have been expended, and by three o'clock, you feel that you have to use your reserve tank to carry you through to five o'clock. At five or six o'clock in the afternoon, you feel that your energy reserves have been exhausted and that all 100 kilowatts of the energy you started with have been used. By the time you get home, your energy reserves are already in overdraft.

People often tell me their families are what really matter in their lives, that family is the reason they work so hard and strive to get ahead. But what the members of our families usually see is a person too emotionally and physically exhausted to have anything left to give. This is a real problem: our family usually gets only a small part of our energy, even though they are the reason we work so hard every day. What most people want at the end of the day is some peace and quiet. *Give me my own space now! I just want to relax and have some peace!* Does that sound familiar?

We feel so weary that all we want to do is chill out, sit in front of the TV, with no demands or interruptions. After a couple of hours of peace and quiet, we hope to have once again built up a small store of new energy for spending with our families.

Inevitably, our partners have also had a challenging day, so it is no wonder that nerves are often frayed, and conflict and arguments are lurking just beneath the surface of every comment and situation.

The daily cycle of energy depletion and renewal might seem to be an unavoidable part of life. But in fact, you can break the cycle. By changing your outlook, you can rid yourself of the heavy load that so depletes you and better manage your energy.

Things You "Have to" Do Each Day

Time. It's the one thing each and every person, rich or poor, has in equal quantities each day. No matter who you are, each of your hours still contains only sixty minutes, and each day contains only twenty-four hours.

❖ To examine your relationship to time, do the following exercise: spend a minute or two writing down all the things that you believe that you have to do tomorrow, from the minute you wake up until you go to sleep at night.

When we do this exercise in my seminars, the room suddenly becomes silent, except for the frantic scratching of pens and pencils on paper. People start writing like crazy! Your list might look something like this:

6:00 AM	Wake up
6:05 AM	Get up and brush teeth
6:10 AM	Shower
6:25 AM	Make coffee
6:30 AM	Wake up kids
6:40 AM	Read the paper
7:00 AM	Eat breakfast
7:15 AM	Leave for work
8:30 AM	Read e-mail
8:55 AM	First meeting
10:00 AM	Second meeting
12:30 PM	Have lunch with John
1:40 PM	Buy birthday card for friend. And so on.

Now examine your own list. Notice that every single item on it has the potential for stress if not accomplished. But that potential for stress can be removed by changing how you relate to each of the items on that list.

There isn't anything that you *have* to do!

Once again, the concept of choice is critical. By *choosing* to do things rather than feeling that you *have* to do them, you will be able to give 100 percent of yourself, and you will discover that your entire relationship to what you do will be different. No matter what your list looks like, no matter how many important things you underlined and decided that you absolutely have to do the following day, you actually don't *have to* do anything. Not brush your teeth, read your e-mail, or have lunch. Think about it.

What You Do Is Up to You

People feel powerless because they think they *have to* go to work, *have to* play with their kids, *have to* love their partners. But, in fact, you don't *have* to do any of these things!

When you wake up in the morning, for example, you actually have a couple of choices. One of them is to stay in bed; another is to get out of bed and go to work. Remember that the choice is always yours, and with every choice, there are consequences—some perceived as positive and others as negative.

If you choose to get out of bed and go to work, you must remember that you alone made this choice. As you'll recall, there is nothing that you *have to* do!

The problem is that most of us are oriented to the *consequences* of our actions (or lack of action), and this orientation drives our behavior. Instead of asking, *What is the right thing to do?* we look at the possible consequences of our choices and decide, *Ooh, I don't like that consequence; that will make me feel pain! So I'd better do it/ not do it!*

We go immediately to how we will feel about the consequences, instead of truly considering the right thing to do. Because we may not like the consequence of one choice, we forget that it is, in fact, optional. You don't *have to* go to work just because your boss will be

angry if you don't. She may indeed *be* angry, but it is stil
for you to choose to go or not.

The fact is, you can choose to do what you want in
When you come from a vertical perspective, you exercise your free
will, the power of choice that we all have. You have control over your
life when you empower yourself by exercising your power to make
choices.

Balance and Dynamic Tension

You cannot fully activate your power if you are constantly
distracted and not aligned with your inner vision. I often hear people
say that they wish they had more balance in their lives because their
current state of affairs is filled with unwanted tension and stress.
When prompted for a deeper explanation of what they really want,
they express their discontentment with how long or how hard they
are working and/or the lack of time they have with their families even
when they are at home.

In fact, what they really want is to have their cake and eat it too.
They want to achieve success in their chosen field (by focusing their
energy on it) *and* have the discretionary time to be with their family,
go for hikes in the forest, and do whatever their heart desires. We
all need to accept that when we choose to focus more energy in one
area, it will mean less time, energy, and focus in another area. The
important thing to remember is that *you* are choosing where to be,
when to be there, and with whom. Remembering this choice should
alleviate any conflicted or resentful feelings. Understand that living
a balanced life really means feeling at peace with your own time
allotment rather than fitting into some 50/50 time-share program
that you feel is the social ideal.

**"Balanced" is highly individual; you are balanced when *you* feel
you are in a state of equilibrium (or well-being).**

The real question that we should be asking ourselves is, *How can
I achieve the results that I want and also enjoy these results?*

When people feel they are out of balance, they feel that their
energy is wasted, not fully utilized. This causes them to feel conflicted,

which leads to stress and problems both at work and at home. This stress, in turn, impacts on their physical, emotional, and mental health.

So, we understand *why* it is important to have a feeling of balance. Now let's look at a practical way of *how* to achieve it.

How to Achieve a Sense of Balance

The key to achieving a sense of balance is to remember, once again, that you are the chooser. If you choose to be *here*, give 100 percent right now, without complaining or wishing that you were somewhere else. If, on the other hand, you wish to be *there*, go there and give 100 percent there, without complaining about wanting to be somewhere else. That is the key.

For instance, when you give 100 percent at work in everything you do and focus 100 percent on how to improve those things you do, you feel engaged, committed, and have a strong sense of purpose. When you finish work, you are satisfied because you have taken responsibility for your choices, actions, and consequences. Since you are the one who *chose* to go to work, you feel energized and empowered.

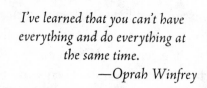

> I've learned that you can't have everything and do everything at the same time.
> —*Oprah Winfrey*

Conscious Compartmentalization

Being conscious of what adds the most value wherever you are enhances relationships both at home and at work. We feel we have more energy in the day when we use the energy available to us wisely. Overall, we feel much happier with ourselves and have a far more positive outlook on life, other people, and things around us.

The mistake that many people make, with resultant lack of balance in their lives, is that they don't compartmentalize the different areas of their lives. This can lead to lack of closure when they come home from work. The pressures and activities of the day keep their minds occupied and focused on work, even when they are at home. Instead of giving their family 100 percent, they might share only 20 or 40 percent, because the other 60 or even 80 percent is still processing issues from work.

When this continues day after day, week after week, month after month, their energy is drained, and they are in "system overload"; they are increasingly stressed and ultimately feel that their life isn't as it should be.

The following exercise will help you to achieve a sense of balance through a process of conscious compartmentalization that shifts the focus from your work life to your home life in a way that values both.

❖ When you finish work and "choose" to go home, evaluate your day at work. For the first half of the journey home, ask yourself questions such as:

> *What really worked well today?*
> *At which point of the day was I really "on"?*
> *What did my quantum magnet attract today at work?*
> *What didn't work so well today?*

Then ask:

> *What is my action plan for tomorrow at work, so I can improve the things that did work well and change or stop doing the things that didn't work well?*

In other words:

> *How can I fine-tune my quantum magnet so that what I am giving each day adds more value not only to me but also to those around me?*

Once you have taken care of work for the day and have a clear action plan for what you will do at work tomorrow, you will have a sense of completion regarding this area of your life. Then, you can start directing your focus toward your home life. This ensures that you do not take work home with you and are able to give 100 percent at home to your family.

During the second part of the journey home, ask yourself these questions:

> *How will I contribute to my family when I get home?*
> *How can I add more value to my partner today?*
> *How can I add more value to my children today?*

Because these questions are constructive, your creativity will start to flow, and you will find yourself generating a wealth of ideas. Questions like these not only foster a positive general mood and attitude that will rub off on others but also lead to small yet caring acts. Your way of adding value at home does not have to be huge, just simply meaningful and purposeful.

**Make a conscious point of asking how
you can contribute more, today.**

By making a conscious point of asking yourself how you can contribute more to your home life and then applying the answer in a practical way, your energy will multiply when you are at home or with your friends. You will also find that this frees you to devote yourself entirely to work when that is the appropriate thing to do. You are free from the nagging sense that you are spread too thin, and you find you have a far greater sense of well-being.

Must We Allocate Equal Time to All Aspects of Our Life?

Time is an important component of balance, but it's not the only component. We don't necessarily have to divide each day into eight hours for work, eight hours for sleep, and eight hours for the rest of our life.

We could spend ten hours at work and only two or three hours at home with our family before the children go to bed, and our life could still be in balance. Of course, this only holds true if we give 100 percent of ourselves to home when we are at home.

Balance and Health

Earlier in this chapter, we touched on the effects of stress on our health. When people feel out of balance, their quantum magnets attract adverse types of energies and emotions into their lives, causing conflict. As a result, they start feeling even more anxious, fearful, and insecure.

When we allow our ego to direct us to horizontal "reactions," catabolic adrenaline is released into the body. This is a *toxin* for organs and cells, suppressing the immune system, leading to weakness and poor health.

When we live a balanced, vertical life, however, anabolic endorphins that have a *tonic* effect on our organs and cells are released in the body. This strengthens our immune system and enhances vitality.

Toxic or tonic? The choice is yours.

The Power of Perspective

Understanding that you *choose to* rather than *have to* do things, makes a powerful difference to your sense of equilibrium and well-being. This simple change in perspective enables you to accept things in your life more easily. Rather than feel victimized, you gain a real sense of personal strength. You thus *choose* to love your children, *choose* to stay in your relationship, and *choose* to go to work. You are the ultimate chooser in everything that you do.

> *Until you value yourself, you will not value your time. Until you value your time, you will not do anything with it.*
> —*Scott Peck*

Knowing that we have made the choices in our lives changes our whole mental attitude, disposition, focus, and energy. Indeed, it changes our whole relationship to work. A 2002 Gallup research study shows that over 70 percent of employees in the United States are not engaged at work: that is, they really don't want to be there! Such a low level of engagement makes it clear that they are not going to work because they choose to but because they believe they *have* to.

Turning this situation around is so simple. We can all change the meaning of work from having to (for survival) to choosing to (in order to create a better life for ourselves, our families, our customers, and communities). Taking things one step further, we can even see it as contributing to the future of all who will be impacted by what we are creating at work.

This awareness immediately changes our relationship to work. It enables us to be 100 percent engaged in what we are doing, so we can give the very best of everything we have to give. Our creativity flows, and we are passionate about what we are doing; we feel alive, and we connect better with others.

Furthermore, at the end of the day, we take home with us the positive energy that we experience at work. Imagine what that does to our domestic happiness and satisfaction! We aren't bringing our work back with us. Rather, we bring our positive energy to share with our families. We are in balance, and the whole effect is self-sustaining. When we are refreshed by our enhanced home lives, our work performance improves significantly, and the rewards from that performance follow. These rewards, in turn, stimulate even better performance. The astonishing thing is that nothing about the situation has changed.

The right attitude is more than just the power of positive thinking. It's about *big-picture thinking*, which we can only do when we are coming from a vertical perspective.

Amazing how a change in perspective can change your whole life!

Perspective and Performance

At work, in relationships, at home, even in our leisure activities, we often ask ourselves, *How can I improve my performance? How can I become more successful?*

Usually we answer ourselves with, *Let me change my behavior.* But, based on your own experience, do you find this easy to do? For most people, it is not. It's very tough to change behavior, especially when it has become a habit.

The next thing that we do—sometimes simultaneously—is to try to change our *attitude*. We've all heard people tell others to stop being negative and start being positive. But again, based on your experience, how easy is it to do this, especially when you are entrenched in a negative mind-set? Not easy. When we're feeling negative and things just aren't going right around us, it's very difficult to be positive.

The final thing that we do to try to improve performance is to get motivated. As you will know, this, too, is possible but usually short-lived. If you are already unmotivated and feel down, it isn't easy to change your level of motivation instantly.

It is clear that behavior, attitude, and motivation are all very important, but in and of themselves, they are not enough to achieve better results.

So, what is the missing piece? Is there some kind of secret formula for accelerating human performance? From all my years of working with people, I have found that the explanation is much simpler than it's made out to be.

The "Outlook Shift" Formula

Geneticists work very hard at cracking the genetic DNA code, hoping to understand the genesis of disease and thus prevent it. For some years, I have focused on trying to understand the code to human outlook. Through my interactions with thousands of people, I discovered what I call the outlook shift formula, an insight that has the potential to create a substantial and permanent shift in our lives.

It works like this.

The *outlook* (thoughts, beliefs, and views) that you have on life shapes your *motivation* (how you feel), which impacts on your *attitude*, which then shapes your *experience*, which in turn influences your *behavior* (how you act), which ultimately impacts the *outcome* and the results you achieve.

Outlook—Motivation—Attitude—Experience—Behavior—Outcome: it's a powerful formula and can be applied to anyone, at any time, in any situation or circumstance.

By changing your outlook, you inevitably change your outcome.

Many studies have shown that almost all weight loss diets fail within the first two years, despite the billions of dollars and countless hours that North Americans spend each year trying to lose weight. How can this be?

What it tells us is that people are focusing on their behavior, attitude, and motivation, but they haven't changed their outlook. Their perspective or relationship to food, their bodies, and their health remains largely unaltered. And so, most weight loss is not long lasting or sustainable. Change in *outcome* can only occur when there is a change at the start of the chain in *outlook*.

We can initiate change by changing our outlook (the way *we* choose to look at things), and, thereby, ignite the chain reaction process of the outlook shift formula, making change or transformation much easier. From the essential starting point of a change in outlook, everything else flows: motivation, attitude, experience of events, behavior, and outcome. Figure 7 illustrates how your choice of outlook can dramatically influence your outcome, setting you off on a path of horizontal failure or vertical success.

Turning the Outlook Switch

Seeing the big picture, living vertically is not just a matter of psychology and abstract theory: it involves practical actions that we can use to turn around our life situation. Which brings us to the next question: *How do I shift from a small-picture outlook to a big-picture outlook (i.e., from a horizontal mind-set to a vertical mind-set)?*

Recall what we looked at in chapter 5, and remember our discussion on choosing the vertical response. We saw how it is possible to stop an automatic reaction by choosing a conscious response instead. Here we examine the process in more detail, starting with three interdependent steps that are essential for making the vertical shift:

> Step 1: Be physically at ease and mentally alert
> Step 2: Acknowledge the stimulus
> Step 3: Align the response to your purpose

Be Physically at Ease and Mentally Alert

The first step is to be alert and attentive to what is happening around you, while remaining physically relaxed—being mindful. We need to open our eyes and ears, to heighten our senses, and be aware of all that is happening around us. When we are fully aware, our perspective is broad, and we are able to examine all aspects of the situation.

Figure 7

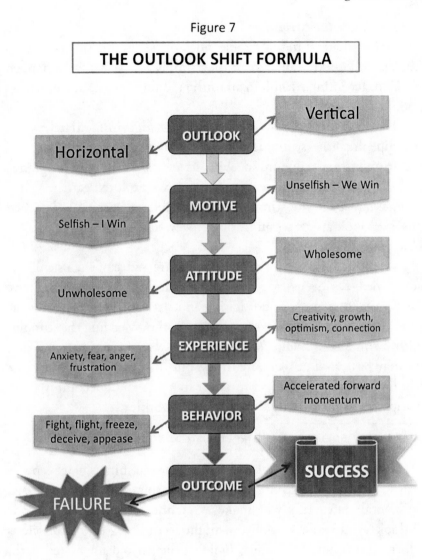

THE OUTLOOK SHIFT FORMULA

OUTLOOK — Vertical / Horizontal

MOTIVE — Unselfish – We Win / Selfish – I Win

ATTITUDE — Wholesome / Unwholesome

EXPERIENCE — Creativity, growth, optimism, connection / Anxiety, fear, anger, frustration

BEHAVIOR — Accelerated forward momentum / Fight, flight, freeze, deceive, appease

OUTCOME — SUCCESS / FAILURE

If you have seen the movie *The Matrix,* you will remember how the action sometimes slowed so that the hero was able to see a bullet coming and have time to get out of the way. In a way, that's what we are doing here: the bullet is the external stimulus. When you are fully conscious and alert, you can slow the path of an incoming stimulus to give yourself time to examine it and acknowledge it for what it is.

Acknowledge the Stimulus

Unfortunately, many people operate on automatic pilot, in a kind of robot-like state, where they simply allow things to happen to them, accepting stimuli in an unfiltered form, without wondering about their effects.

The second step, then, is to acknowledge immediately what is happening (the stimulus or trigger); this creates a gap between the stimulus and your mind, with its neural paths and programs, and stops the automatic reaction pattern we explored earlier. When you acknowledge the stimulus, you are able to become a detached observer, look at the stimulus objectively, and consciously choose a new path.

What a difference it makes when we are aware of each stimulus, acknowledge it in a neutral way, and see it for what it is. We then have the power to stop old conditioning in its tracks, even by using the simple technique we saw earlier—simply acknowledging the stimulus with a smile or a silent, *Thank you for sharing!* On any given day, we may have to do this many times, but this practice will illustrate just how we are exercising our power to choose and becoming more competent at identifying the ego and its workings.

Acknowledging your "triggers" stops your ego in its tracks.

In short, in step 2, you make sure that the mind's gatekeeper is on the job and thus avoid the downward spiral into the ego-based horizontal state. This will make a remarkable difference to your outlook. And while, initially, it might seem like a lot of conscious effort to examine a stimulus, switch from an old unwanted path, and respond from a vertical perspective, rest assured that the process eventually becomes easier. We have to ensure, however, that the chooser is "awake" at all times because the ego is also alert and busy developing new strategies.

Align the Response to the Purpose

Steps 1 and 2 made you alert and able to acknowledge the stimulus for what it is, giving you enough time to dodge the bullet by asking yourself, *What does that mean?* and *How should I respond?*

Now you have reached step 3, the most important part of the process of shifting your outlook: how *do* you respond?

By allowing yourself the time to respond to these questions in a conscious manner, rather than react to them horizontally (which could taint your response with anger, frustration, resentment, fear, or anxiety), your response can come from your authentic self. This is a positive way of responding, one that leads to contentment, inner peace, happiness, and further growth. You respond by aligning your response to who you want to be: that is, a vertical being with a particular purpose.

❖ To help anchor your response to your greater purpose, examine your answers to the three pivotal questions:

1. What is *my* purpose here?

In chapter 2, we examined the importance of defining your life purpose. This purpose is the foundation for everything that happens in your life, which includes determining your response at every moment. If you don't have a clear vision of your purpose, or if you are not fully committed to that purpose, the rest is all empty theory. If you aren't already completely sure about the answer to this question, refresh your memory by going back to the exercise you did to determine your purpose. Your purpose needs to become such an integral part of who you are that your main focus every day is simply to align your outlook, feelings, and actions with that purpose.

2. What is *their* purpose here?

We must remember that we are not responding in isolation, and, therefore, we also have to consider from where the other party comes. It is important to ask yourself this question in reference to others who are involved in the incident/event or situation that has become a trigger. We need to be aware that, deep down, they may have similar desires to ours but go about achieving these desires in a different manner. Perhaps their intentions are good, but they may also just be stuck and not know how to get what they want.

3. How can I contribute?

Finally, we need to decide what role we can play in achieving our purpose and contributing to others. We need to ask questions such as, *How can I help?* and *What can I do?* The answers to these "other-focused" questions will help guide your response in a positive way.

These three pivotal questions reinforce the *creation of a gap* between the stimulus and the response. This gap allows us the time to get into the right frame of mind from which to choose the most vertical response. Asking these three questions strengthens our ability to acknowledge the stimulus, examine it, and decide what is best to do with it, as we take into account our own purpose and that of others. In this way, we can confidently decide how best we can contribute.

> *This is the true joy in life: the being used for a purpose recognized by yourself as a mighty one; the being a force of nature instead of a feverish, selfish little clod of ailments and grievances complaining that the world will not devote itself to making you happy.*
> —*George Bernard Shaw*

Imagine what the world would be like if the actions of all nations and peoples came from the point of view of what they could contribute.

No Attachment

An essential element of this process of transforming your outcome through your outlook is feeling secure with uncertainty. We cannot know exactly how the new outcome will unfold.

When we are in the midst of a transformation, we don't know what is in store for us or the people around us. What we do know is that it will be fresh and new, and that we will evolve into people who are more confident, courageous, and resilient.

We recognize that the full picture of what this new life will ultimately look like is incomprehensible to us before we start. This unknowing and our open, trusting state is what makes transformation so exhilarating.

Chapter 7

Be the Chooser

You have now seen how a simple change in perspective—from I "have to" to I "choose to"—can cause an extraordinary shift in your outlook. Again and again, we come back to the underlying theme of free will. We will now see that, in truth, the most unfaltering tool that we have available to us as sentient beings is the power of choice: the choice of how to respond, how to behave, and how to live. Realizing that you are the "chooser" in your own life is the key to authentic power.

When you understand that *you* are the chooser in your life, and when you decide to exercise that freedom of choice, you will be conscious of the control you have over your own destiny. This awareness brings true power to situations where you once felt powerless. You cannot control how other people behave, but you *can* choose how to respond to their behavior. You *can* choose to resist your habitual and unconscious reactions, and instead, choose a positive response that will result in a more positive outcome. You can choose to activate your own power.

Control vs. Constriction

Once you realize that you are always the chooser in every aspect of your life, you will also realize that blaming anyone else is giving away your power, making yourself a victim. In order to experience your true power, you need to take full responsibility for your choices and actions, as well as for the consequences that will arise from those choices.

If you believe that your life is controlled by external forces and you choose to react from a small-picture, horizontal perspective, you will feel restrained and restricted, forced into a bubble created by those forces. In such a confined space, your problems and worries will soon occupy the entire room. Before long, you may start to feel desperate, gasping for breath and smothered by everyday problems and minutiae.

The irony is that people usually make this choice—opting for the small-picture, horizontal alternative—because they feel that this is the *safe* choice. But as our worry and anxiety grow, the narrow and restricted perspective becomes the *least* safe option. When things don't happen the way we want them to, and when we feel that someone else has the power to decide our fate, we feel more and more anxious, more restrained, more miserable.

In this situation, this constrained bubble, the focus of life becomes maintenance and preservation rather than the creation of something positive. When we live this way, we are likely to feel threatened and suffocated every time something negative happens. And at the back of our minds, we know that it's only a matter of time before something happens that triggers that reaction again, since our lives are subject to control and manipulation by outside forces. It goes without saying that living in such a vulnerable state is very uncomfortable and unpleasant and not something that most people would choose consciously.

Victim Mentality

There are always a few obstacles waiting around the corners of your life's path, but it is your relationship to those obstacles that determines your happiness. Do the following statements sound familiar?

The reason my marriage didn't work is because of my domineering mother-in-law!

I can't get promoted because my supervisor doesn't appreciate what I do!

I am overweight because those fast-food companies keep advertising super-sized versions of their meals!

These examples may seem ridiculous as you read them, but they are real. You have probably heard them, maybe even said them, in one way or another. Whether it was the exact words or exact "excuse" shown here doesn't matter; the underlying mentality is what counts. People who don't take responsibility for their own lives and their own actions are said to have a victim mentality.

How can we tell when somebody has such a mind-set? It's simple. They reveal themselves when they constantly blame or criticize others. If we continuously blame others, we haven't accepted our responsibility. If we criticize and complain, we haven't taken responsibility.

Choose Your Response

❖ Think about something that has happened recently between you and another person that made you angry, frustrated, irritated, or upset, something that still has emotional energy attached to it. Remember how you felt and how you reacted. Did you choose to play the victim role? What was the outcome?

Perhaps you recalled a negative event such as your teenaged son answering your friendly greeting with a dismissive grunt, or perhaps your manager failed to acknowledge the fact that you worked late every night for a week. You may have found that your temper rose, and you reacted in a way that was not in line with your normal behavior or desired values. If so, you allowed yourself to have a negative experience through your own small-self reaction to the event.

All events in our lives present us with a choice to accept or resist. It is important to remember that at any time and under any circumstance, you are the chooser, with the power to control how to respond to any event.

Figure 8 illustrates the two alternative paths that we follow in resisting or accepting what is. It is clear that very different consequences result from choosing horizontal (small-self) thinking versus vertical, big-picture (higher-self) thinking.

At the center of the diagram is an "Event," which can be any event in your life—from losing your job to something trivial such as misplacing your reading glasses—as long as it initiates an emotional reaction in you. It is important to note that most events are simply that: events. They are neither negative nor positive *until we think them*

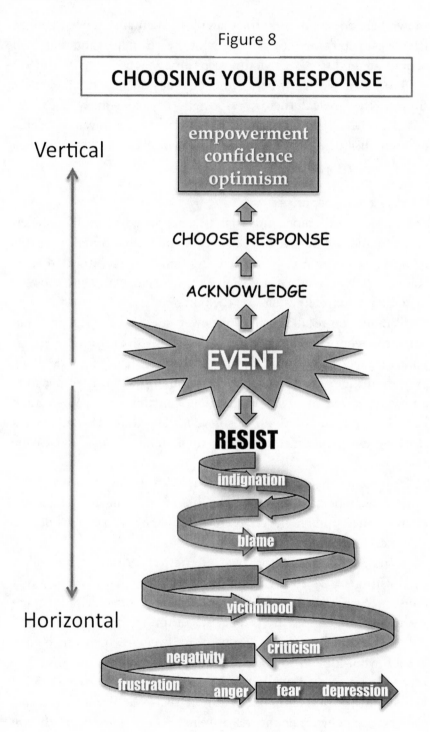

Figure 8

CHOOSING YOUR RESPONSE

Vertical

empowerment
confidence
optimism

CHOOSE RESPONSE

ACKNOWLEDGE

EVENT

RESIST

indignation

blame

Horizontal

victimhood

criticism

negativity

frustration   anger   fear   depression

so! It is our emotional reaction to an event that leads to arguments and raised blood pressure.

An event can only control you if you allow it to.

Negative (Horizontal) Response

Look at the sequence in figure 8 where the chooser responds to an event in a negative way, spiraling downward. The first thing that most people do when something negative happens to them is to resist it and express their feelings of indignation: *"It's not fair! It's not right! How could you do such a thing? Why did you do that to me?"*

When we choose to react this way, the next thing that usually happens is that we immediately blame someone else: *"It's her fault! It's him! It's them!"*

Sometimes we even blame ourselves. In short, we do not take responsibility for being the chooser in reacting to the event.

Finally, our victimhood leads to other negative emotions, which we experience in the form of frustration, pessimism, anger, fear, or anxiety. Worse still, instead of putting aside the event after its occurrence and moving on, most people store the experience and its associated feelings as ammunition for a future occasion, such as repeated conflict in a relationship. Before long, when something negative happens again, these unresolved issues are triggered and the downward cycle continues.

Each time we repeat the cycle, we resist with even more force and blame with more conviction and self-righteousness. We give the

> *Our experience is not what happens to us, but what we make of what happens to us.*
> —Aldous Huxley

whole process more and more energy, and all that happens is that the issues keep growing and generating even stronger negative feelings and emotions. Sometimes the event itself is almost forgotten, while the emotions take on a life of their own. We feel unhappy, anxious, and unbalanced.

When Events Take Away Our Power

Most of us continue on this downward spiral until our survival mechanism kicks in and something inside us says, *Enough is enough! I'm going to suffocate unless I do something!* When we heed this warning signal, instinct propels us back onto the survival track. Like the cork in our example earlier, when forced beneath the water, we follow our instinctive mechanisms and bob back up above the surface to gasp for air.

Sometimes we think we've solved the problem that was gripping us in the downward spiral, but unfortunately, most of the time we have merely temporarily suppressed it to find relief. And so we continue our old up-and-down, up-and-down cycle of existence.

Have you ever experienced a situation in a relationship where a contentious issue takes on an energy of its own and grows and grows, like a monster? When this happens, neither party in the relationship is in control. It's the event itself—or rather, the situation and the emotions it generates in us—that takes on a life of its own. Whatever we suppress grows, and everything we resist persists. So, by resisting, we ultimately feed the event or situation with more energy. We give the event power over us.

When this works through both partners in a relationship, both partners experience the negative consequences. If we continue to spiral down into the deep horizontal level, with all its negative emotions and consequences, we harbor increasing animosity, frustration, anger, and all the trouble that accompanies such feelings.

This is when we give away our power. And when we give away our power, we also negatively impact on everyone we come into contact with—particularly those we love.

Taking Back Your Power

When we react to an event by choosing a lower-level reaction, we get a downward spiral of blame, negativity, and escalating anger. By contrast, when you accept that you are the chooser, you realize that you can just as easily choose to respond from the vertical perspective.

When we recognize that we have the power to choose in any situation, we need not wait for others to make decisions for us. We refuse to act like powerless victims of circumstance. We do our utmost to do the right thing. We take back our power.

The alternative to chronic vulnerability is to choose to live in a vertical state and to see life from the big-picture view that this perspective reveals. This is what it means to be the chooser of your destiny.

Choosing the vertical perspective removes us from the downward spiral.

When we consistently choose to live life vertically, we find that negative things don't seem to have as much effect on us any more. We feel more calm and confident. Our capacity to deal with problems is far greater, and from our new, big-picture perspective, most of these issues seem small and insignificant.

Imagine that due to the downturn in the economy, your company has decided to lay off a certain percentage of its workforce. Senior management has announced that they will let everyone know what the new structure is going to be and who will be part of it and who will not within a week. Suddenly, you are faced with the reality that

> *Nothing in life is to be feared, it is only to be understood.*
> —*Marie Curie*

you may lose your job. From the small-picture perspective, it is a dreadful shock. Even if you were confident in your value as an employee, it would be hard not to feel less valuable or worthy. From this perspective, finding another job would be a very daunting task because you would feel frightened, insecure, vulnerable, or inadequate.

If, however, you were able to avoid feeling diminished by the same situation and could open yourself to the idea of losing your job, you would see that suddenly more possibilities would come into existence. And while the experience would still be a shock and would still require action on your part, you would discover that you had some choices you didn't think you had. You might feel lightness and freedom at the prospect of a new and unknown path opening before you. You might even feel anticipation—like having a present waiting to open at Christmas.

The big-picture perspective allows us to dispassionately observe what has happened, and rather than be suffocated by it, look out, up, and around and start choosing again. The process might still be scary, but moving forward with courage in the face of fear shows us new opportunities and makes our world a bit bigger every time.

Choose to Acknowledge

Look at figure 8 again. Note that even though it starts with exactly the same event, you can decide to react very differently and choose a higher-level response. The vertical response begins when you acknowledge that the event happened. This might sound simple, but it is very important, since it immediately puts you in the observer/ witness position rather than in the emotional place of one who is experiencing the reaction. From that removed position, you are able to see the situation more rationally and with greater clarity.

Acknowledgment doesn't mean you don't feel angry or unhappy about the event. But instead of immediately reacting to it in a way that you might later regret, you just step back and see it for what it is. You start by acknowledging it without judgment.

Did the event happen? *Yes, it did.* Did it make you feel angry or unhappy or sad? *Yes, it did.*

You don't resist the event; you just see it for what it is. And instead of allowing an automatic and immediate reaction, one that could lead you on a downward spiral, you are now fully in control. You have opted to activate your power and to be a conscious chooser in this situation.

The next step is to ask yourself, *What would I choose to do about this event or situation or circumstance from a more vertical perspective? How would I then choose to react to this?*

Events can only control you if you allow them to. The key point to remember is that you may have little or no control over what happens to you, but you always have total control over how you *respond* to what happens to you.

A Tale of Two Choices

Imagine you are sitting in your car at a traffic light, and a car comes up too fast from behind and crashes into you. There is no way that you have any control over that. Apart from not being there, in the wrong place at the wrong time, there is nothing you could have done to avoid the crash; you had no control over the accident. You can, however, control your response in order to avoid sinking to the horizontal level: the whirlpool of anger, blame, frustration, and out-of-control emotions.

After the initial shock of a car crashing into you, there are a number of possible reactions available to you. You could, for example, get out of the car and start screaming at the other driver: *You idiot! You could have killed me! Where did you learn to drive—in a bumper car? I'm going to sue you! Look what you did to my car!"* This is small-self stuff: anger, frustration, fear, negative emotions. This type of response not only gets us more entrenched in our own ego, it also usually triggers the other person's ego response. This is how wars start.

On the other hand, you could choose to stay in control of your response and rise above the situation. You could breathe deeply, count to ten in order to calm your emotions, and say a silent prayer of thanks that nobody in your car was hurt. Then you could calmly get out of the car and make sure the other person is okay. You could talk to the driver respectfully (being conscious of the shock that he or she could be experiencing), calmly take the necessary details, and politely wish each other well.

We can always control how we choose to respond to what happens to us.

Can you see the difference in the choice of responses? The first took us to the small self, to the downward spiral of blame, anger, conflict, and out-of-control emotions. And what effect do you think that would have on the driver of the other car? Soon, you both would have been reacting in ways that would give the incident more and more negative energy and potentially allow it to spiral out of control.

On the other hand, a vertical response takes everyone to an entirely different place. By first stepping back and acknowledging the incident without judgment, you can choose your response instead of letting it simply follow an old conditioned program.

Did the incident itself change from the vertical perspective? Not at all. Would you still be shocked, shaken, and upset if you got hit by a car while you were innocently stopped? In all likelihood, yes. But the crucial difference would be that you chose to retain your power in the situation. You chose an elevated, vertical path rather than the downward spiral of the small self.

Long after I considered the above example, I was actually witness to such a vertical response in my own neighborhood. I was walking down the street with my daughter when I heard the horrendous sound of a car screeching to a stop. I turned to see an oncoming car swerve to try and avoid another car that had just run through a stop sign. Although he slowed, he couldn't stop, and I saw the inevitable crash. The young man who had run into the car at fault was visibly shaken when he got out of the car, but his first response was to ensure that the older woman who had failed to stop her car was okay. Luckily, she was also fine, and they exchanged insurance details almost amicably. Neither one of them expressed any anger or blame. I was most impressed to witness such a high-level response and exchange between two strangers in a potentially very tense situation (not to mention thankful that my daughter and I had remained out of danger ourselves).

Changing from Horizontal to Vertical Momentum

If you feel that you may already have entered into a downward cycle, it is still possible to move to a more vertical response. One way to do that is to cease telling yourself the same story over and over in countless conscious and unconscious ways that just keep you stuck. Instead, you can exchange the negative story for your ideal story.

❖ The following ten-step process is designed to help you break the momentum of the horizontal cycle by examining and then releasing the "story." The whole process can be done in fewer than ten minutes. Recall an episode that still carries negative feelings for you.

Step 1:   Focus on the story of the event and notice where in your body you feel the fear, worry, and/or stress.

Step 2: Notice the experience that you have labeled as fear, worry, and/or stress, and give it a size, color, or shape. For example, perhaps you see it as small and oval shaped.

Step 3: Step into that energy and be it. Immerse yourself in that sensation, color yourself with the feeling, or blend yourself to the shape.

Step 4: Step out of it and witness it.

Step 5: Repeat steps 3 and 4 (this will help you develop the ability to move in and out of these experiences at will).

Step 6: Let it *be*. Change *your* relationship to both your story (thoughts) and your emotions (thoughts expressed in your body) by letting everything be as it is. Don't judge the story or your feelings, try to change or manipulate them, or pass commentary on what they mean or how you feel about them. Continue to do step 6 until you can feel a shift in energy. That shift should be a feeling of calm, neutrality, and heightened awareness.

Step 7: Now, visualize your ideal situation. Tell yourself the story as you would ideally want it to be, and put yourself in that new position by seeing, hearing, and feeling the accompanying sensations as though they were happening now.

Step 8: Amplify the senses of sight, sounds and feelings in your mind to anchor that state for yourself.

Step 9: From that newly empowered state, list your skills and talents, and explore the alternative solutions available to you.

Step 10: Choose the alternative that you think would best serve you and those who are affected by that decision. For example, in response to the scenario of layoffs outlined above, you could consider:

Alternative 1. *I will look for a new job.*

> Alternative 2. *I will start my own business in … as I have always wanted to do.*
>
> Alternative 3. *I will wait and see what the changes are and then decide what I want to do.*
>
> Alternative 4. *I will go and work with my brother-in-law, etc. etc. …*

In a vertical momentum cycle, we face the real issues, deal with them, take action, and begin to experience visible results. This energizes us because we feel that life is working for us; our actions are bringing us positive results. We feel more optimistic, empowered, and resourceful, and realize that when we take action, positive results begin to appear. Before long, we start to gain momentum. We achieve more of the results we want—and feel more encouraged, more energized, and more motivated to continue charging that magnet. And so, the vertical momentum continues in an upward spiral.

> *There were always choices to make [living in the concentration camp]. Every day, every hour offered the opportunity to make a decision, a decision which determined whether you would or would not submit to those powers which threatened to rob you of your very self, your inner freedom, which determined whether or not you would become the plaything of circumstance.*
>
> —*Victor Frankl*

In order to activate the vertical momentum, we need to be flexible; we need to be prepared to let go of the old ways in which we have been operating. We need to come from a place of admitting that we don't already know everything. We need to be humble and open.

André Gide, a French critic, essayist, and novelist, said, "Man cannot discover new oceans unless he has the courage to lose sight of the shore."

You cannot continue to do things the old way and expect new results. Most people have heard this before yet continue to do the same things again and again, even when they don't deliver what they really want. You have to be prepared to make some real changes in how you live your life. That is why flexibility is so important. If you are rigid and inflexible and your attitude is always, "I'm fine," when, in fact, things are not really going well at all, you will deny yourself the chance to change anything simply by refusing to confront reality.

To change from the horizontal momentum to the vertical momentum, we first need to confront our own reality.

How Can I Be Sure to Choose the Vertical Response?

Is there anything else you can do to ensure that you will make the right choice and respond vertically and not just slip automatically into an old limiting reaction?

This is the big challenge. My experience has shown that there is a simple but fail-safe three-step process that we can follow for any event. I use this formula constantly and have found that when I respond to any event following these steps, the outcome is always more favorable than it would have otherwise been.

Decision Making in Three Steps: Accept, Change, Exit

Once you start thinking consciously about your response to everyday events, you will find it easy to follow this three-step process. When you do it often, you will find that it becomes an automatic process, an ingrained habit or way of thinking.

❖ Each time that you find yourself confronted with an event, stop and consider your three decision-making alternatives: accept, change, or exit.

Step 1: Accept

At this first stage, you need to ask yourself the question, *Can I accept this (event, situation, comment, etc.)?* If the answer is yes, move on; carry on with your life without further thought. Remember, if you accept, you are not resisting, so there is no pain. It is very important though to understand that to accept does *not* mean that you still resist in some way, or that you accept grudgingly. If a staff member "accepts" his manager's decision to attend a meeting that he was not particularly interested in but hisses under his breath,

"Yes, well, I suppose I'd better go and do what she says," this is not acceptance—it's resistance.

In short, you need to have full and total acceptance, even though there might be some negative aspects involved. You may *accept* fully, for example, as follows:

> *I accept my job, even though the supervisor doesn't treat people very well.*
>
> *I accept this relationship, even though I know that it's not perfect.*
>
> *I accept my lifestyle, even though it's not like a scene out of a movie.*
>
> *I accept my work and the choices I've made, even though they sometimes cause me difficulty.*
>
> *I accept that I've made the choice to stay here, even though the place I came from may seem better in hindsight.*
>
> *I accept my partner, even though we disagree from time to time, because there are more positive aspects than negative.*

Once you have decided on full acceptance, you can have peace of mind and move forward. You need not even go to Steps 2 or 3 because they will no longer be necessary.

If, on the other hand, you decide that you are *not* willing to accept a particular situation, you need to go to Step 2.

Step 2: Change

When you are not willing to accept a certain situation, you can ask yourself the following question: *If I am not willing to accept this, what needs to change?* Maybe *you* need to change your own attitude or behavior; maybe the other person involved needs to change his/her attitude or behavior. Maybe both of you need to change. Maybe you need to take up a new hobby, accept help, put aside time each day just to listen. Maybe you need to state your needs clearly or have the other person do his or her best to meet those needs.

Whatever it is that needs to change, make a commitment to do it and do it wholeheartedly. Too often people make commitments to themselves to change (like New Year's resolutions) and then get disappointed when the inspiration wears off, the required actions don't follow, and the results are not achieved. This applies to relationships at work as well as at home. I often see people committing to working more collaboratively with coworkers and then getting sidetracked by their own ulterior motives and agendas. Change cannot take place without conscious effort and consistent action.

The chances for real change are best when all parties in the relationship can agree on what needs to change and when all parties involved follow through by making the necessary changes and genuinely supporting each other. When real change occurs, you can then move back to unity, cohesion, and growth.

There are times, however, when people say they are going to change, and may even have the intention to do so, but don't really follow through on their intentions. In the case of failure to change, for whatever reason, you are faced with another decision. You can either go back to Step 1 and accept that things are not changing and come to terms with the situation, or you can go to Step 3.

Step 3: Exit or Remove

The question that you need to ask yourself at this stage is *Who needs to exit or be removed?*

At Stage 3, you make the decision that something is no longer workable for you, such as your working conditions, for example, or your unbalanced lifestyle or your relationship. Since you are not willing to accept the situation as it is, and you have tried everything in your power to change the situation (or yourself) without satisfactory results, you are faced with a final choice: either you accept that things are not going to change, or you "exit" or otherwise remove yourself from the situation.

For example: if the problem is at work and you are unwilling to accept the situation in its current form, and you have done everything in your power to make the necessary changes but to no avail, you exit or remove yourself from that situation (i.e., you resign, transfer, let go your disengaged and underperforming employee, etc.).

Figure 9

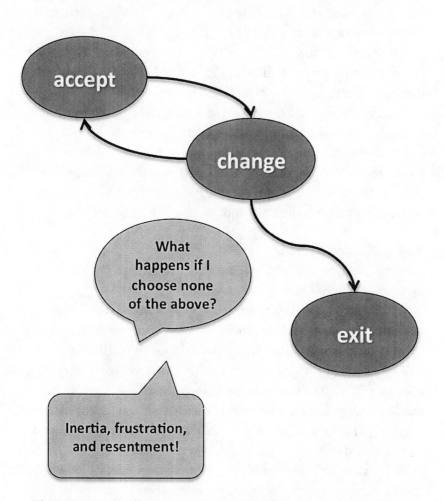

This approach allows you to remain fully in control. You are expressing your personal power by choosing what you are willing to accept and what you are not willing to accept. This experience is very empowering, especially when it aligns with your purpose, your values, and your principles.

> **I activate my authentic power by taking full responsibility for myself, my actions, and the consequences that arise.**

Some people may think that Step 3 is harsh. But consider the alternatives, such as being miserable at work for years on end or staying in a relationship where both parties are perpetually unhappy, even after they have attempted all possible avenues of reconciliation. Remember, too, that the sequence of the steps is accept, change, and *then* exit/remove. Moving straight to *exit* is not a wise or suggested option!

The Consequences of Choosing "None of the Above"

The biggest problems arise when people are not willing to accept the situation on the one hand, but on the other hand, they do not change what is not working and nor do they exit or remove. Not surprisingly, they continue to resist, blame, and feel frustrated, unhappy, and victimized. Feelings of resentment and disrespect toward others begin to build. They criticize and put down other people, find fault with many things that others do, and take their frustration out on them. In short, they project their own unhappiness onto the world.

When we fail to choose Step 1, 2, or 3, and, instead, do nothing, we choose a very destructive route. We hurt ourselves and create a lot of pain and suffering for people around us. Our inaction lowers our level of consciousness: it squashes us into the horizontal perspective. It starts to sap our energy and that of others. We poison not only ourselves but everything with which we come in contact.

Sadly, this non-option is what many people choose, and this is why so many people experience negativity and unhappiness in their lives. They stay stuck in a discomfort zone of their own making. They neither come to terms with the situation and accept it, nor make the decision to change and do everything they can to make it work, nor decide that things simply aren't working so someone needs to exit. Instead, their choice is *inertia*—and then they wonder why they feel unhappy, stuck, and frustrated!

The next time you are faced with any decision, remember your options: accept, change, or exit/remove.

Chapter 8

Be Real

Is there anything still standing in your way, preventing you from activating your full power? Surely, once you have shifted your outlook and realized your power to direct your own choices, you should be free to act in the service of your own highest purpose.

Remember our old nemesis the ego? The ego, our biggest obstacle to realizing our true potential, can actually take on a whole life of its own, creating its own personality, which serves as your public face, and derail even your best efforts. To truly realize your full potential, you have to recognize this artificial construct and detach yourself from the need to maintain it. Then you can give direction to the choices you make by examining your own core values and asking yourself who you truly are and what you really stand for.

Bondage to Your Self-Created Image

Have you ever wondered why some people feel totally confident in some situations, but in other situations, they appear insecure, vulnerable, and fearful? How can they seem confident one day and insecure the next?

What is it that causes people to feel so insecure? Why do they take great pains to conform? Why is it that so many people are afraid of what others think of them? And what can they do about it so that it's not an issue in their lives anymore?

For a long time, I couldn't understand why it seemed that we have so many seemingly incongruent parts to us. Then one day, during one of the leadership programs I was facilitating, I noticed that some of the senior managers were feeling uncomfortable during their feedback presentations to their peers and leaders. It suddenly became clear. I realized that it isn't standing up in front of people (or speaking to them) that is the real issue for most people. Rather, it is our fear that other people (especially those whose opinion of us we value the most) will think less of us than how we *want* them to think of us. This insight allowed me to see what an enormous effect the gap between our own self-image and the image we want to project (our "desired" image) has on how we think, feel, and act.

Your Desired Image

Look at figure 10, and imagine that the person on the pedestal is the person you want the world to see, the self you have constructed for public view based on all the external input you have received, either consciously or unconsciously, over the years. In fact, this is your ego on display, doing whatever it can to survive and look good.

> *The most common ego identifications have to do with possessions, the work you do, social status and recognition, knowledge and education, physical appearance, special abilities, relationships, personal and family history, belief systems, and often political, nationalistic, racial, religious, and other collective identifications. None of these is you.*
> —Eckhart Tolle

As we grow up, we get told a lot of things by parents, friends, teachers, and the media. They tell us who and what we should be, how we should look and dress, how we should behave in order to attract favor, and to avoid ridicule and criticism.

From a very young age, therefore, we are conditioned to behave in a specific way. We are told that unless we do this or be that, we will be rejected and unhappy. Even after we've grown up, society continues to tell us what we should be, how we should look, and how we should behave. Advertising and the media play a large part in social conditioning in our adult lives, as do our social circles.

In essence, from your earliest days, you have continually been investing in your external image or public persona. Unconsciously, you have constructed a persona that belongs on a pedestal, someone that meets the needs of your loved ones or your society, someone you now have to strive to live up to!

Figure 10

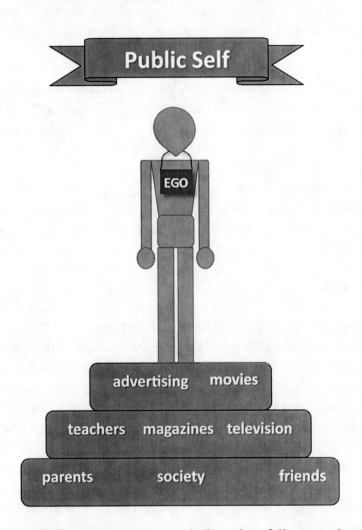

CREATING THE DESIRED IMAGE

The self-created image includes the following kinds of aspirations:

I want the world to see me as the best son, the best husband, an ideal father and employee/manager, smart, successful, intelligent, and so on.

or,

> *I see myself as this attractive person, the best daughter, the best mother, the most romantic lover, the dynamic career woman, smart, successful, intelligent, and so on.*

Most people need the world to see that they are a "somebody." And because we have made such a huge investment in this persona we have created, we feel terribly threatened when it is questioned or attacked.

We Will Do Anything and Everything to Protect Our Image

We protect most strongly what is most valuable to us. The bigger our investment, the bigger our attachment—and the higher the value we place on it. The measures we will take to protect valued things are accordingly greater.

It's no wonder, therefore, that every time there is a risk that our investment in our self-created image might be compromised, we feel anxious and defensive. We fear that people might see us as we really are, instead of seeing the image we wish to present. Even on a subconscious level, this is an extremely strong force, one that can lead to massive aggression and conflict when triggered.

The Gap Between the Desired Image and the Real Me

In contrast to our "desired" image is the "real me"—the authentic self. Because we have invested so much in our desired image, some of the real me has inevitably been suppressed. This may mean suppressed from everyone, even from our own conscious minds, or from all but a select few (perhaps a few trusted people are allowed to know the real me). We all know people who are very different once we have gotten to know them well enough for them to be comfortable and reveal their true selves. But in their public lives, when they are at work or in social situations, they strive to display their desired image (public persona). This creates enormous tension and inner conflict because the public performance requires a lot of energy.

Think about it: when there is a gap between our desired image and the true self, we are constantly afraid that other people might see through the game that we are playing. We feel threatened, even if only subconsciously.

This helps to explain why so many people fear public speaking. It is hard to understand why an otherwise competent person suddenly has a fear that she might make a mistake and not know what to say. Or why another person fears that people might laugh at him or that the whole situation might turn into a disaster.

This is the ego in operation. The real fear is that the slightest mishap could compromise the carefully constructed image, so the ego creates all these little supporting fears *(What will happen if I forget what to say? What if I stumble or my voice shakes?)* to disguise the real fear *(What if other people suddenly see through this mask and discover the me that is vulnerable, nervous, and not perfect; no one will believe anymore than I am confident and self-assured!).* Faced with all these potential disasters, we naturally feel threatened and insecure.

Sadly, we spend an immense amount of energy sustaining our exterior image, even though it's just a façade, a looking-good game. When there is a gap between our desired image and the real me, life is exhausting. Every time we are with people, we have to spend energy trying to maintain our façade, trying to look good and making sure we say the right thing, rather than being authentic and real. And because we feel threatened, we try to protect this image and if necessary, justify its existence. When we are self-protective, our ego kicks in, and we experience anxiety and often react defensively when questioned. The bondage to our desired image creates unhappiness and prevents us from experiencing inner peace and harmony.

So, What Is the Solution?

To attain the vertical perspective and activate your power, you must first set yourself free from the control and bondage of your desired image. Furthermore, we must liberate our real selves from the conflicts and negative outcomes that go with our attachment to this image.

To become totally comfortable with being the real me, we have to get to a point where we are not dependent on other people's opinions. We need to replace our ego-based motivation to be seen and perceived in any particular way with a deeply felt aspiration live up to the highest expression of who we *really* are. When the no longer a gap, there can no longer be inner conflict. No more will we have to expend energy thinking about how we "should" look or behave or what we should be saying or doing.

Absolute Confidence

Once you are comfortable with your real me, the biggest advantage is that most of your fears will melt away. If you are not self-conscious, you are no longer afraid of what people might think. You will then find it easier to connect with others and relate to them in an authentic and carefree way.

Being real removes fear.

Although most of us (to a greater or lesser degree) care about what people think or say about us, the difference in confidence comes, once again, from an understanding that we have the power to choose how to respond. When we activate this confidence, we are no longer intimidated by internal questions such as, *Do they like me? Will they accept me? What will they think?*

Confidence is directly linked to your authentic self and, therefore, is the confidence of being who you really are: secure, fulfilled, and powerful. Internal, authentic confidence imparts the feeling of being alive without any attachments, conditions, or expectations. This is living in the vertical mode.

In the horizontal mode, your confidence is always relative: relative to the situation, relative to how you feel, and relative to what is happening in your life right now. In the vertical mode, the confidence you experience is not dependent on external situations, conditions, or circumstances. Your confidence arises from within.

> *We are so accustomed to disguise ourselves to others that in the end we become disguised to ourselves.*
> —*François Duc de La Rochefoucauld.*

You no longer need to waste energy by continuously maintaining an image or trying to be what you think society wants you to be. You feel liberated! You cannot be rejected without your consent. You cannot be criticized without your consent. Remember what we saw in chapter 7: you are the chooser at every moment of your life.

When you actually assume your power to choose and the responsibility you carry for all your own actions and their consequences, your confidence will come. From that position of strength, the vertical momentum generates even more power. Power is self-sustaining.

Clearing the Path to Freedom

We have seen so far that clarity comes from being sure of and committed to your purpose, and also from viewing life from the big-picture (or vertical) perspective. Still more clarity comes from facing everything (your emotions, your fears, your own ego) and thus, feeling the freedom of having nothing to hide.

While we are going through this process, it's vital to make sure that you deal with the issues that arise and clear them out of your way to allow free passage to your goals and desires. It is not necessary or recommended to delve exhaustively into your personal history, but

> *It is better to be hated for what you are than to be loved for what you are not.*
> —André Gide

rather, to reframe it and look at it from different perspectives. By doing so, you will re-own or re-identify with parts of yourself that you have disowned or suppressed, and this will, in turn, enable you to free yourself from these recurring issues.

Clarity comes from facing everything and feeling the freedom of having nothing to hide.

The following exercise gives us a peek at how we can free ourselves from the bondage of the limiting and elusive ego that prevents us from experiencing our whole self.

❖ This exercise, *"See Everything and Avoid Nothing,"* helps give clarity to your own multifaceted self:

Step 1: Think of an issue or person that has been bothering you, and hold it in your mind.

Step 2:   Describe the situation, person, or feeling from an "observer" position. (For example, you are a bystander, not involved at all, who observed the situation and who is currently being interviewed by a journalist reporting on the incident. What would you, as the observer, tell the journalist?)

Step 3:   Next, talk to the person or address the issue from a more involved position: "your own" position. You may want to ask questions such as, *"What is the message that you are bringing me?"* or, *"What are you showing me that I was not able to see before?"*

Step 4:   Now, move into "their" position and *become* the issue or person that has been bothering you. See the situation purely from the opposite perspective, and allow yourself to be open to what you see, hear, and feel.

Step 5:   Finally, embrace all three perspectives and integrate them into one "whole you." Now, experience what it feels like to see and understand things from all these perspectives and parts of yourself.

The Power of Reality

When you have a disappointing experience in your life—your relationship, work, or business—you probably feel compelled to do something about it. However, when you don't approach the issue from the vertical perspective, but instead let your ego deal with it reactively, problems arise.

When we approach setbacks or disappointments from the horizontal perspective, we look for external solutions, anything that will take away the pain and make us look and feel better. Many people deal with this discomfort by looking for scapegoats (who may have nothing whatsoever to do with the actual event). By dumping their anger and frustrations on someone else, they can relieve themselves from their own pain and discomfort. This behavior provides temporary relief, but before long, another event presents itself that triggers those uncomfortable and angry feelings again ...

and the cycle continues. These destructive behaviors and lose-lose outcomes have played out throughout the history of mankind: when we read the newspaper or watch TV and see the continual conflict between people and nations, we see it still today.

External solutions can never be the real answer. While they might bring some temporary relief, they have no long-term power. When we rely on external solutions to our problems, we are only perpetuating the ego momentum. We feel we are really working hard at solving our problems, and we are trying everything to reverse the downward trend and to achieve good results, but because our perspective is restricted, we are really just patching up an emotional wound with a Band-Aid. The truth is that nothing from the outside can heal an emotional wound: only healing from the inside can reverse the momentum of the downward cycle.

> *Always be a first-rate version of yourself, instead of a second-rate version of somebody else.*
> —*Judy Garland*

When we get rid of our attachment to the desired image, we become real. And when we become real, we move away from the heaviness and complexities of the horizontal perspective into the vertical mode of simplicity, inner peace, excitement, and passion. We feel alive and present, neither dwelling on the past nor obsessively worried about the future.

When you are true to yourself, you will find it easier and easier to face difficult situations that crop up and find a resolution for them. Because you are no longer invested in an ego-created public self, you can focus all your energy on the issues at hand. Not only is this empowering, it leads to clarity, contentment, and a feeling of being at peace with yourself.

Chapter 9

Share Your Gifts

In previous chapters, we examined the importance of giving 100 percent to achieving a sense of well-being, balance in our lives, and authenticity in our behavior. But there is another reason for giving 100 percent. By giving fully of yourself, of your particular gifts or talents, you also activate your power through the strength of generosity and the magnitude of abundance. How can we ensure that we always feel abundant, rich with time, love, and energy? By recognizing how much we already have, by appreciating what we have now, by being truly grateful, and by sharing and contributing to others' well-being.

If we give 100 percent of our love, this indicates that we have 100 percent of love to give. The same holds true when we give of our time, passion, or energy. When we share 100 percent of who we are, in everything that we do, our quantum magnets are activated and attract more of that powerful and positive energy back to us. The positive energy that we gave out is returned to us from other sources, so we can continue to share what we have. Giving creates abundance, which stimulates more giving: an example of positive momentum!

When our intention to give comes from having so much to give in the first place, it is unconditional. When we give unconditionally, we are truly contributing to the world.

Stop Waiting

Many people feel that there is always something missing from their lives because they are seeking solutions from the outside, when in fact, as we have seen, most answers come from within. People, therefore, look futilely for better relationships, better jobs, more money, and more things in the hope that these will resolve all their issues. Even when they achieve these goals, most people still don't feel fulfilled.

It is possible to strive to develop yourself and achieve more while simultaneously being grateful for what you already have, but most people merely focus on what they don't have and wait for something better. What they are actually saying is, "*This moment is not good enough*"—which means, "*I am dissatisfied*"—which leads to a belief, "*I don't have enough.*" This all adds up to a state of ungratefulness, unhappiness, and lack of fulfillment. In this state, no matter what you have, it seems that there is always something missing.

Being Grateful

❖ For a few minutes, think about all the things you are grateful for in your life right now. How does it make you feel? Did you notice that thinking about being grateful brings you fully into the present? Did you notice the feeling of abundance it brought you?

Better still, did you notice how gratefulness made you feel calm and at peace? And isn't it wonderful that when we focus on feeling grateful for all the things we have and are, we forget about being resentful for all the things we don't have or aren't?

I have found this to be such a valuable exercise that I recommend doing it several times every day. We all know how the minute we get to work and the phone starts ringing, everything changes, and it is very easy to get distracted. That's when our habitual negative responses can be triggered.

To ensure that the power of gratitude lasts all day, we need constant reminders and reinforcement of the fact that we are grateful.

Express Your Gratitude Each Day

❖ Each morning when I wake up, I ask myself what I am grateful for in my life right now. And each morning, I go through some of the things that I am truly thankful for:

> *I'm grateful that I have this additional day to live.*
> *I'm grateful that I can see and hear and talk and walk and smell and feel and taste.*
> *I'm grateful that I have the power to choose in every moment.*

I'm grateful that I love and am loved.
I am grateful that I have a supportive and caring wife.
I'm grateful that I have three magnificent children.
I'm grateful that I am able to work in a profession that I love.

This gratitude exercise is obviously unique for each person. But, by expressing our gratitude as individuals, we all gain in a similar way. That is, we focus away from, and above, our own problems and issues.

Many people have told me that by doing the gratitude exercise each morning, they start the day feeling totally energized, grounded, and at peace. I do this exercise every morning when I wake up. My other favorite time to do it is when I am crossing the bridge on my way home from downtown Vancouver to the North Shore, driving straight at the beautiful, often snow-capped mountains. The surge of positive emotions, the feelings of joy, fulfillment, and peace that well up as I make my way across the bridge deck remind me each time that I have been blessed to be who I am and do what I choose to do. I am fully aware of the beautiful and peaceful environment that I live in and how fortunate I am to have something so compelling to go home to—my family.

You will note that in my grateful exercise list above, and probably in yours, too, there are very few references to material things. We don't usually think of these things when considering what we are truly grateful for. Therefore, almost anybody in any part of the world, no matter what his or her level of prosperity or material well-being, can follow the same basic gratitude exercise and experience the same feelings of peace and joy.

With gratefulness and conviction of abundance, we feel rich.

When the gratitude exercise becomes your daily practice, you will see that it is difficult to be in a bad mood or to have a bad day. You will have a new perspective on how lucky you are, and you will discover new value in what you might formerly have taken for granted.

Like the ad says, reminding ourselves that we have so much to be grateful for: priceless!

Relationships Without Gratitude

Without gratitude, the feeling that something is missing in our lives usually extends into our personal relationships.

As we saw in chapter 4, like attracts like, so we initially choose people because we can relate to them—and they choose us for the same reason. Thus, for the first few months in a new relationship, everything seems to be perfect. We think about each other all the time, we do everything together, we feel alive, fulfilled, and excited. We put on our finest clothes, fuss with makeup, use our best language and manners, and we are on our best behavior. We phone each other five times a day when we are apart, and just can't get enough of each other when we are together. Like the old cliché, we are two hearts beating as one.

Yet, after a while, this euphoria wears off. Suddenly, we don't feel quite so wonderful. Instead, we feel a kind of separation taking place. We start examining the relationship from our habitual small-self perspective, which says, *Don't lose your identity in this other person! The only way to survive and get your way is to be separate.* So, we find ourselves having little arguments and noticing faults where previously we only saw perfection.

This is when we start saying things like, *"You don't tell me that you love me anymore. You don't respect me enough. I'm putting more into this relationship than you are! You don't appreciate me!"*

Sound familiar?

We worry that the relationship is not as good as it used to be. We feel that the other person does not care for us like before and that there must be a problem in our relationship. We start to blame the other person for not living up to his or her side of the deal. We blame the other person for our own lack of fulfillment.

Do we simply accept that this is just the way all relationships are? Or is there an alternative to this pattern?

In our relationships, as in life in general, things do not have to be so dissatisfying. We can choose to live *with gratitude*. Instead of self-protective scrutiny of the relationship, gratitude helps us to focus on what is right. Remembering what we are grateful for within the other person helps us remember what we loved about them in the

first place. This change in
outlook removes us from our
isolated, small-self perspective.
It is difficult to complain
when we are basking in the
glow of appreciation for the

> *As we express our gratitude, we
> must never forget that the highest
> appreciation is not to utter words, but
> to live by them.*
> —*John F. Kennedy*

other. And like so many other things we have discussed already, this
shift in perspective creates a positive feedback loop: your partner will
appreciate you for appreciating him or her.

No More "Taking for Granted"

Being grateful is a beautiful gift when expressed to someone else.
I invite you to express your gratitude now to those people who are
precious in your life in a way that allows them to experience your true
love, true appreciation, and true thankfulness for your relationship
and your connection with them. And remember: love in action is
much more meaningful than mere love in words. The combination
of those two, however, is magnificent.

One of the biggest benefits of gratitude is that it prevents us from
being overly concerned about ourselves and our problems. It helps us
to live more consciously and to remember that we have the power of
choice. It stops us from wavering continuously between the past and
the future. For a few moments, we become present; we stop being
self-centered and become more other-centered. We no longer worry
about "what is missing," because we are focused on what we have.
Self-absorption falls away, and we begin to contribute in ways we
never really imagined possible.

Being grateful in each moment is about being thankful for all
the moments in our lives. It is about valuing life itself. In the movie
Forrest Gump, one of the most memorable statements that Forrest
made was when he said, "Life is like a box of chocolates; you never
know what you are going to get." Well, we, too, don't know exactly
what we are going to get, which is another reason to exercise gratitude
for what we already have.

The Power of Forgiving

In order to be in the state of mind needed to feel truly grateful and to give more of yourself, you first need to relieve yourself of negative energy that may consciously or unconsciously be holding you back. Forgiving others of any wrongdoings, true or even just perceived, will pave the way to freeing yourself from bondage to negativity.

> *The desire for revenge is a heavy chain, and revenge itself leads to a chain reaction. Forgiveness cuts the chain.*
> —Margaret Atwood

True forgiveness creates relief. Relief from holding onto energy that is destructive in nature and fosters resentment, anger, and hate. It takes courage to forgive. People who can find that courage, though, feel more liberated and at peace with themselves.

Forgiveness does not mean consent or complacency. It is a compassionate act, rather than acceptance or agreement with what has, or has not, happened. We can forgive without implying that it will be okay if it happens again.

Think of a time when you forgave someone and how it made you feel. Many people hold onto issues from their past relationships with parents, friends, or partners that consciously or unconsciously weigh them down and diminish their sense of well-being.

Below is an exercise that can help in clearing the way to giving fully of yourself. You can do it in your mind or on a sheet of paper. I find that writing it down is more helpful, since it allows me to see it in front of me, rather than getting lost somewhere in my mind.

❖ Answer the following five questions:
1. What is the biggest rock/issue/challenge that I am carrying in my life right now?
2. Why is it important for me to clear this issue?
3. How will resolving this issue help me to achieve my goals and align myself with my purpose?
4. How will resolving this issue benefit others?
5. What actions will I take in the next forty-eight hours to get started?

Doing this exercise regularly will make you feel lighter and more at ease. In turn, this will give you the freedom to express yourself fully in your relationships with others and, ultimately, connect at deeper levels.

Forgiveness is empowering, a constructive act that allows you to finally put down your rock.

A wonderful poem on forgiveness was found written on the wall of Mother Teresa's home for children in Calcutta, India, and is widely attributed to her:

People are often unreasonable, irrational, and self-centered.
  Forgive them anyway.
If you are kind, people may accuse you of selfish, ulterior motives.
  Be kind anyway.
If you are successful, you will win some unfaithful friends and
  some genuine enemies. Succeed anyway.
If you are honest and sincere people may deceive you.
  Be honest and sincere anyway.
What you spend years creating, others could destroy overnight.
  Create anyway.
If you find serenity and happiness, some may be jealous.
  Be happy anyway.
The good you do today, will often be forgotten.
  Do good anyway.
Give the best you have, and it will never be enough.
  Give your best anyway.
In the final analysis, it is between you and God.
  It was never between you and them anyway.

The Ego's Reaction to Giving 100 Percent

When we choose to give 100 percent, the natural reaction from the ego is usually a big no! The ego part of us is selfish and wants only for itself. At times like these, it's crucial to remember that *you* are the chooser and that *you* have the power.

The challenge we face is that sometimes, even when we are alert and attentive to external triggers, these triggers can still challenge us.

And when our ego is challenged, we often feel strong emotions that influence us to give in to its urges and insistent demands.

Remember, you can enroll the ego in helping you achieve your goals rather than allowing it to steer you off course by following the steps we have been through in the previous chapters.

Create the gap that allows you to assess the trigger by acknowledging it when it appears. With these few extra seconds, take the time to recall that you have the power to take charge, and you don't have to react unconsciously and automatically.

> *He (or she) derives strength not from what he gets out of things and people, but from giving himself to life and to others. He discovers the secret of life in the creative energy of love—not love as a sentimental or sensual indulgence, but as a profound and self-oblative expression of freedom.*
> —*Thomas Merton*

Ask the questions that distinguish between your higher purpose and the ego's purpose: *"What is my higher purpose here?"* and *"What is my ego's purpose here?"* Once you are clear on your purpose, you know with certainty what you need to ask next: *"How can I express my purpose in practical terms to contribute and add value to others?"*

Thwart your ego: refuse to harbor resentment.

Your ego will not get the better of you if you are alert and attentive, and you will be able to give what you want to give.

But What's in It for Me?

So, what *are* the benefits for each of us in giving in this way? First, the mere realization that you have 100 percent to offer is a gift in itself. Second, fully sharing your gifts means that you will experience abundance yourself. You will no longer feel that something is missing from your life; you will feel free and boundlessly generous.

When you choose to give 100 percent in every moment, not only will you attract more of the same positive energy, but you will also fill that moment completely, without being distracted by the future or the past. You will experience what it's like to be totally present and fully alive.

A few years ago, I attended a live performance of the master violinist Itzhak Perlman. The theater was packed with people in great anticipation of a marvelous concert. The maestro entered the stage, bowed to the audience, acknowledged the orchestra, and began to play. Within two minutes or so, I began to feel something that I had never experienced before at any concert I had ever attended. I felt a shift in my awareness and in an instant became fully present and at one with the sound that was vibrating in my head and body. Tears started rolling down my face, and I almost magically entered a state of awe, bliss, and gratitude. The musician and the instrument had become one, and I had been invited to enter their communion. I experienced what I can only imagine was the maestro's experience when he became one with his music. I remember my wife looking at me and realizing what was happening and, with a gentle smile and a twinkle in her eyes, she acknowledged my joy.

After that experience, I realized that one of the key reasons people like to watch masters in music, sports, and other areas is to feel that heightened state of presence. They rejoice in the experience of the masters becoming one with the ball, puck, or musical instrument. One of the main reasons why people become so unhappy, angry, and frustrated with their "heroes" when they are not performing at their best, is that their expectation of entering that state and having that experience has not been met. One of my lessons from my orchestra experience was that the only way for me to enter into that state is to remain open and receptive to it, rather than expect something or someone external to do it for me.

Abundance vs. Scarcity Mentality

When you have an abundance mentality, when you believe that there is plenty around for all of us, your quantum magnet will attract more abundance. You will exude energies that express abundance, and you will attract energies that generate prosperity and affluence in your life.

If you come from a scarcity perspective, on the other hand, you will experience scarcity, and wherever you look, there will be lack and dissatisfaction. When we expect the worst or the least, our quantum magnets will attract just that.

When we read the headlines in the newspaper or on the Internet with a scarcity mentality, that scarcity worldview is reinforced. Everything around us seems consistent with what we focus on. And what we focus on impacts how we express ourselves in the world.

The collective scarcity mentality was clearly displayed during the last economic downturn, when many corporations started experiencing a slowdown in their business and, with the influence of the media frenzy stimulating their own fears, overreacted. The trust within these organizations was lost, and the fear of the employees intensified, leading to a further drop in productivity and performance.

> Gratitude is riches.
> Complaint is poverty.
> —Doris Day

Interestingly, the leaders of a few organizations managed to rise above the noise and capitalize on opportunities others were not able to see. The external event (economic downturn) was the same, but the way that it was experienced was different. So, what determines scarcity or abundance? Our perspective does. And who determines our scarcity or abundance? Since we are the choosers in our lives, we do!

Prosperity Is a Choice

Each day, I look at my environment in the beautiful city of Vancouver, British Columbia, and I see high-rise buildings, luxury cars, beautiful homes, restaurants, magnificent parks, and resorts. There is evidence of abundance and prosperity everywhere.

And yet, living in this same city are people who don't see that prosperity and, therefore, don't share in it. Although they may have ended up in that position through misfortune, nobody has to stay there. Each of us, no matter what our circumstances, has the choice to improve our condition—or not. This is not to say that everyone 's equal opportunity or that the playing field for success is at all fair.

No matter where you are in life, it is very important to recognize that your own self-limiting beliefs and lack of commitment to your purpose are almost certainly holding you back from your own success, whatever that may mean for you.

If you are not living the life you want, if you do not have a feeling of abundance and prosperity (no matter what your actual economic or social circumstances), you are coming from a scarcity mentality. It makes no difference what you tell people, or whether you work hard, attend seminars, or read self-help books: if there is a part of you that has a scarcity mentality, or that believes that money is evil, for example, that is what you will focus on and experience more of. Scarcity is what you will attract.

Prosperity mentality is just that: a mentality that gets you to see the abundance and richness of life, nature, and your surroundings. It is not based in hard reality or external materialism, either, but rather in the way that we choose to look at our world. You can have a mentality of prosperity and live a life of abundance and satisfaction even if your actual economic means are limited, just as you can live a life of scarcity and lack when you are actually in the upper economic strata.

Change your perspective, and you change your life. Look deep within, and determine whether you have a mentality of scarcity or abundance. Mindfully begin to nurture a prosperity consciousness by focusing on, acknowledging, and appreciating the abundance that you see around you.

Let's Revisit the Horizontal and Vertical Perspectives

Where do sharing your gifts and understanding the scarcity or abundance mentality fit into the earlier work we have done? Go back and take another look in chapter 2 at figure 1, which shows the horizontal and vertical perspectives.

At the extreme horizontal level, where people have a scarcity mentality, the situation is lose-lose. This means that people who are at that level are there because they view the world (and hence experience the world) in ways that create scarcity, misery, depression, and in extreme cases, hopelessness. Not only are they losing out on the gifts that life offers, people around them may also be losing, their energy being drained by proximity.

At the normal horizontal level, most people still operate from a moderate scarcity mentality. They function through fear and craving and, therefore, still have many selfish motives. We call this the I win mentality. That is, most of life revolves around "me": *"As long as I get what I want, I'm okay. If others around me get what they want, that's just a bonus."* What people are really focused on here, when we scratch beneath the surface, is ensuring that they achieve what they are striving for, without true consideration of the needs of others.

> *I am of the opinion that my life belongs to the whole community, and as long as I live, it is my privilege to do for it whatever I can.*
> —George Bernard Shaw

When we get to the vertical level, where the perspective and outlook is that of abundance and caring, we call this win-win or we-win (myself, the other party, everyone else). The key focus at this higher level is that *everyone* involved wins, and this applies to every situation, no matter what the circumstances. Think Mahatma Gandhi, Mother Theresa, Martin Luther King Jr., and Nelson Mandela: their focus was *world-centric* rather than merely egocentric. Equality, freedom, and a sense of dignity for all of humanity were their common goals. You may feel it is unreasonable to expect the rest of us to live up to the accomplishments of this exceptional group of people, but really, all that each one of them did was to make a choice to do the right thing. The rest followed. They were all fully committed to a higher purpose, which extended beyond their own self-centered needs.

In the words of Martin Luther King Jr. himself, "If a man hasn't discovered something that he will die for—he isn't fit to live." This sentiment—in different words—was also expressed by Mahatma Gandhi; it shows their commitment to giving 100 percent of themselves with the main purpose of creating a better world for all.

Tuning Your Quantum Magnet

You may be questioning whether you can change your own perspective so that you can attract what you want. How *can* you realign or tune your quantum magnet so that it will attract abundance and more positive things into your life?

The entire process we have been following throughout this book is designed with that outcome in mind. By taking the steps toward activating your power, and by committing to live a more vertical life, you will begin to realign your quantum magnet with your true nature—your higher self. Above all, in all situations and under all circumstances, you must consciously and consistently be aware of what you are thinking, feeling, doing, and attracting.

You may find that part of you feels impatient with this process and wants to rush through, skip the "smaller" steps, and just get to the outcome! Perhaps you skipped over the exercises and read ahead quickly to find the "trick" or directions to the path to instant success. Ego generally does not like repetition and would prefer to move on to the next thing without anchoring the information needed to become more vertical. In fact, your ego doesn't *want* you to become more vertical, since the more vertical you become, the more your ego loses power over you. Take the time (once you have finished quickly reading the book, if this is you!) to go back and do the exercises with full attention.

Our memories hold more when our interest is captured, when we remain open, and they improve through repetition. This book offers different tools and strategies to reinforce repeatedly the changes you need to make to truly activate your power.

Let us, therefore, review our progress from the beginning.

First, you made the decision to become more vertical, identified your purpose, and committed to living in alignment with your self-created purpose. Then you examined your biggest obstacle, the ego, and your greatest ally, the quantum magnet. Next, after considering the role our emotions play, we explored the wisdom of viewing life from a big-picture perspective and of moving away from the kind of unconscious reactions that the small self would take. You committed to taking full responsibility for all your choices, actions, and their consequences. That gave you the power!

Later, you learned to stop being attached to your public face and, without that attachment, were able to shift your outlook from an "I have to" mentality to a purpose-based focus. You reviewed the importance of generosity and forgiveness and resolved to give 100 percent of yourself in everything that you do.

Overall, you committed to living a full life by being awake, alert, and fully in the present.

Can you see how, by diligently following these steps, you will become a master tuner of your quantum magnet? For the next thirty days, at least once a day, check your quantum magnet to determine what it is attracting. If it needs tuning, you know what to do!

Chapter 10

The Time Is Now

Knowledge is power only when it is translated into action. And that is why the final step in activating your power is to overcome any remaining fears and resistance to change and take action. This means that you stop allowing your ego to drive you and, instead, choose the high road, do the right thing, and do it *now*.

Many people have the necessary knowledge for living a more fulfilling life: they are well read, highly intelligent, and may even claim to, "be in the know," because they have read it, seen it, heard it, and done it.

But, based on what we see in most people's behavior (and hear from their speech when they are not censoring their thoughts), it is clear

> *I have been impressed with the urgency of doing. Knowing is not enough; we must apply. Being willing is not enough; we must do.*
> —Leonardo da Vinci

that few have crystallized or integrated this knowledge and experience into their lives in a way that achieves meaningful results.

If we are not living it, it means that we don't really know it. This distinction is very important. It accomplishes little if we have read many books, attended many seminars, listened to good advice, but are not actively creating a better life as a result of such efforts. We will only be able to live our dreams if we have the courage to seize our power and *act*.

Live in the Present, not the Past or the Future

By now, it should be clear that constant worrying about what happened yesterday, or what might happen tomorrow, can be a potent obstacle to activating your power. This constant rocking chair movement between yesterday and tomorrow triggers the ego and activates our fears and insecurities. It prevents us from having the ability to truly smell the roses that are under our noses because our minds are elsewhere.

There is only one place we can live, and that is in the present.

When we live in the now, we are fully engaged in this moment with focused attention, curiosity, and interest. There is no room for worry or fear. When we cease ruminating over what *has* happened or worrying over what *might* happen, we can experience fulfillment, inner peace, and true joy.

Planning, setting goals and having a vision are important because they help give direction to your purpose. However, it is what you do *right now* that will help you reach your goals and attain your vision. There is no such thing as later. Life is now. This moment is your life. You can't live in the future, and you can't live in the past. When you realize you no longer have the burdens of the past or the worries about the future, you can find the perfect peace within yourself—right now.

What happens with many people, however, is that they are *here*, but they want to be *there*. And then when they are *there*, they want to be somewhere else! This constant dissatisfaction—*This is not good enough and I'm not where I should be*—leads to inner conflict, wasted energy, and frustration. This sense of dissatisfaction can also prompt incessant seeking for what we don't already have, which prevents us from ever "finding." Peace is always out of reach when the goal itself is seeking.

When do you know that you are living in the present? When you are truly grateful at each moment and are no longer waiting for anything. This does not mean that you do not need to *do* anything; in fact, when firmly situated in the present, you will find that you are your most creative, passionate, and excited about life.

It is only in the present that you can give 100 percent in everything that you do. Reciprocally, when you make the choice to give 100 percent, you become fully engaged in the now.

There Is no Magic Pill

Earlier in this book, we spoke of some of the obstacles on the pathway to activating your power. One of them is impatience. Many people want things to change without being willing to do much work for it, as if a magic wand could be waved or a magic pill swallowed. They want the results and the success without doing what is required to achieve them. Or, if things don't work perfectly the first time, they simply give up and go back to their old ways.

Once you begin to take the steps that have been outlined in this book, you will realize that although there is no such thing as a magic pill, there is no need for it either. *All the magic lies within you.* But it takes commitment, effort, and inspired action to achieve results.

The bottom line is that change requires effort, and only those who are seriously committed to their purpose will do the necessary work.

Dedication, commitment, and action will bring the changes you desire.

It's like digging for diamonds. You can't decide one day that you want to be a diamond prospector and *presto*, the diamonds appear in your hands. Rather, you have to do some research, buy some equipment, enthusiastically stake out a claim, and remove an extraordinary amount of dirt and rock before you get to a diamond. After a few days of sweating in the hot sun without finding any diamonds, many people would simply pack up. They had their plan and the technique, but when they didn't get instant results, they simply abandoned the project.

Quitting too soon is a huge trap for many people. Progress and results require focused attention and perseverance. But in the end, to quit—or to continue—is *always your choice.*

It is important to know that your resolve will constantly be tested throughout this process of transformation, but if you are aware of the tests and traps, you won't be caught off guard. Also, know that standing by your new choices will not always be easy. Remember the key questions that you need to keep asking yourself: *How serious am I about this life?* and *How much do I really want it?*

The Dots Are Connected

The principles we have discussed thus far are all integrated. You can't choose just one or two of the principles on their own, or use the steps outlined in this book as a smorgasbord, and hope to succeed. Each step builds on the previous one, using it and reinforcing it simultaneously as you become more vertical, more focused.

Your entire existence starts coming into balance once you realize that something fundamental is missing from your life. Then, when you find your highest purpose and make the decision to be clear and committed to it, the clarity you gain allows you to contribute 100 percent of who you are to your work and family.

Viewing life from a big-picture perspective allows you to move away from the kind of unconscious reactions that the horizontal, small self would take and that change in outlook leads to positive changes in outcomes. Furthermore, once you recognize the basic truth that *you are the chooser in your life,* you no longer avoid taking full responsibility for all your actions and their consequences, and thus, you reclaim your power. By not being attached to your old "constructed" or "desired" image, you become free to be your true self. You stop wasting energy on trying to be what you think other people want you to be and so are enabled to be more authentic and vertical.

A vertical outlook allows you to truly feel and express gratitude, a daily practice that, in turn, brings peace and a sensation of generosity and abundance. With an abundance mentality, sharing your gifts by giving 100 percent of all that you are, in everything that you do, comes naturally.

The power is now in your hands. If you are seriously committed to achieving a more purposeful, meaningful, and abundant life, you will start taking action.

More than Anything Else

Start by focusing on what you want, and make that your life's mission. Take another look at the qualities of life that are most important to you (happiness, abundance, joy, peace, love, balance), and adjust the alignment of your purpose.

Fulfillment, joy, passion, and so on are always available to you; if you really want to experience them, you just need to awaken to them and connect with them. You don't need more time. The time is now!

❖ If you are not sure how to proceed, ask yourself three simple questions:

> *What is most important in my life?*
> *Why do I value it?*
> *How much do I really want it?*

When you prioritize exactly what you want in line with your purpose, you will do what is necessary rather than what your feelings of fear and anxiety urge you to do.

The statement, "I want this more than anything else in my life," has more power than whatever else you might be feeling right now. It is powerful enough to override fear and doubts. "*More than anything else*" means more than your ego's needs, your emotions, thoughts, or current situation.

Remember that what you attract into your life is determined by the energy you send out. The more focused your energy, and the clearer the messages that you send out, the clearer the energy that you attract. It is obvious, then, how powerful an impact on your quantum magnet the phrase, "*more than anything else*," can have.

Do the Right Thing

You now possess many practical tools, techniques, and strategies for activating your power. Your ego can no longer trick you by coming

> *Everyone has been made for some particular work, and the desire for that work has been put in every heart.*
> —Rumi

up with any more excuses like, "*You don't know how to do this.*"

In fact, there is only one thing left to do, and that is to do the right thing. That means do it in every single moment, again and again and again.

In most instances, we know what is the right thing to do. The reason we often go in circles is not because we don't know but because we are not willing to face our fears, insecurities, and self-doubt. We are, therefore, more committed to comfort than to our goal.

Don't let your ego use fear to distract you from doing the right thing.

To keep activating your power sustainably, persist in living the principles outlined in this book and following the steps and exercises laid out for you. Otherwise, the old momentum will take over again. You may get energized and inspired for a week or two, but without sustained attention, the conditioned momentum of old habits is such a powerful force that it's almost inevitable it will drag you back down.

> *Until one is committed, there is hesitancy, the chance to draw back, always ineffectiveness ... Whatever you can do or dream you can, begin it. Boldness has genius, power and magic in it. Begin it now.*
>
> —Goethe

Helen Keller, who overcame great adversity and became a role model for millions of people, said that, "Life is either a daring adventure, or nothing." We can either live a life that focuses on mere survival and preservation of the old, or we can choose to live a life where we are continually moving forward and creating something better in every single moment.

A life of preservation is internally focused and self-centered, while a committed way of living is externally directed and considers the whole. The life of mere survival is driven by fears, worries, and insecurities, while a full and creative life is driven by service to others, burning passion, zest for life, and the purpose to create a better future. The first is stagnating; the second is constantly evolving.

We have the gift of life, and with that gift, we have the power to choose how we use it. We have the power to choose our outlook, our motive, our attitude, our behavior, and ultimately, we have the power to choose our outcome. When we realize that we *can* choose, we become the powerful creators of our own destiny. And this, I believe, is the most exciting part of being a human being.

When we consistently choose to do the right thing, we experience a state of "flow." In this state, we experience everything in full alignment. The quantum magnet is attracting positive energy. We experience pure passion, exhilaration, profound creativity, and the ultimate pleasure of being alive!

This Is Your Call to Action

Your life is in your own hands. You have the tools to reshape it in a way that will create more joy, fulfillment, and abundance for you, your family, and for all those with whom your life intersects.

If you are truly serious about this powerful life within your grasp, you will act. Things will happen. Results will be achieved. Trying is not good enough. Be seriously committed to doing it, or not. The choice is always yours.

This is your time. This is your opportunity. Use the gift of life that you have so miraculously received. Go share it with the rest of the world.

I wish you every success in your new adventure.

Recommended Reading

Ageless Body, Timeless Mind: The Quantum Alternative to Growing Old, by Deepak Chopra, Harmony (1993).

The Biology of Transcendence: A Blueprint of the Human Spirit, by Joseph Chilton Pearce, Park Street Press (2002).

Birth of the Chaordic Age, by Dee Hock, Berrett-Koehler Publishers, Inc. (1999).

A Brief History of Everything, by Ken Wilber, Shambhala Books (1996).

Building the Bridge as You Walk on It, by Robert E. Quinn, John Wiley & Sons (2004).

Conscious Evolution: Awakening the Power of Our Social Potential, by Barbara Marx Hubbard, New World Library (1998).

The Ecology of Commerce: A Declaration of Sustainability, by Paul Hawken, HarperCollins Publishers (1994).

Flow: The Psychology of Optimal Experience, by Mihaly Csikszentmihalyi, Perennial (1991).

Good to Great: Why Some Companies Make the Leap and Others Don't, by Jim Collins, Harper Business (2001).

The Holographic Universe, by Michael Talbot, Harper-Collins (1991).

Infinite Mind, by Valerie Hunt, Malibu Publishing (1996).

Man's Search for Meaning, by Viktor Frankl, Pocket (1997).

A Path with Heart, by Jack Kornfield, Bantam (1993).

The Power of Now, by Eckhart Tolle, Namaste Publishing Inc. (1997).

The Power of Your Subconscious Mind, by Joseph Murphy, Wilder Publications (2007).

Power vs. Force: The Hidden Determinants of Human Behavior, by David Hawkins, Veritas Publishing (1998).

The Seven Spiritual Laws of Success, by Deepak Chopra, New World Library (1995).

The Soul of Money: Transforming Your Relationship with Money and Life, by Lynne Twist, W.W. Norton & Company, Inc. (2003).